Canada East

by Fiona Malins

Fiona Malins has many years experience writing travel guides and has specialized in books about Canada and the United States. She has collaborated on a number of AA books, including the AA KeyGuide to Canada as well as books for the National Geographic Traveler series, Fodor and AAA. She ia also a tourist guide and lecturer traveling widely across North America and lives in Montréal.

Above: *Lake Mephrémagog in Québec's Eastern Townships*

AA Publishing

Flute player at Old Fort William, Thunder Bay

Written by Fiona Malins

First published 2005.

© Automobile Association Developments Limited 2005.
Mapping produced by the Cartographic Department of the
Automobile Association.

Published by AA Publishing, a trading name of Automobile
Association Developments Limited, whose registered office is
Southwood East, Apollo Rise, Farnborough, Hampshire, GU14
0JW. Registered number 1878835.

A CIP catalogue record for this book is available from the
British Library.

Find out more about
AA Publishing and the
wide range of travel
publications and services
the AA provides by
visiting our website at
www.theAA.com/bookshop

A01997
Mapping produced from Canada data © Tele Atlas N.V. 2005.

Colour separation: Keenes, Andover
Printed and bound in Italy by Printer Trento S.r.l

Contents

About this Book

This book is divided into five sections to cover the most important aspects of your visit to the region.

Viewing Eastern Canada pages 5–14
An introduction to Eastern Canada by the author.

Eastern Canada's Features
Essence of Eastern Canada
The Shaping of Eastern Canada
Peace and Quiet
Eastern Canada's Famous

Top Ten pages 15–26
The author's choice of the Top Ten places to see in the region, listed in alphabetical order, each with practical information.

What to See pages 27–90
The three main areas of Eastern Canada, each with its own brief introduction and an alphabetical listing of the main attractions.

Practical information
Snippets of 'Did you know…' information
3 suggested walks
3 suggested tours
2 features

Where To… pages 91–116
Detailed listings of the best places to eat, stay, shop, take the children and be entertained.

Practical Matters pages 117–24
A highly visual section containing essential travel information.

Maps
All map references are to the individual maps found in the What to See section of this guide.
For example, Lunenburg has the reference ✚ 29B1 – indicating the page on which the map is located and the grid square in which the town is to be found. A list of the maps that have been used in this travel guide can be found in the index.

Prices
Where appropriate, an indication of the cost of an establishment is given by $ signs:

$$$ denotes higher prices, $$ denotes average prices, while $ denotes lower charges.

Star Ratings
Most of the places described in this book have been given a separate rating:

✪✪✪   Do not miss
✪✪   Highly recommended
✪   Worth seeing

Viewing
Eastern
Canada

Above: *Beulach Bahn Falls, Cape Breton*
Right: *female officers in the Royal Canadian Mounted Police*

5

Fiona Malins' Eastern Canada

Lasting impression
Of all the places I have visited recently, nowhere has made such a strong impression on me as Gros Morne National Park in Newfoundland. Its deep fjords are awe-inspiring, and both its geological features (such as the Tablelands) and its wildlife are exciting. Not only did I see moose and bears during my trip there, but also caribou grazing beside the road.

Right: *Basse Ville, Québec*
Below: *looking out over Bonne Bay, Gros Morne National Park*

I have lived in eastern Canada since 1970, when, as a young immigrant, I reached its shores by ship. After sighting icebergs in the Gulf of St. Lawrence, we sailed up the river to Québec City. I was overwhelmed by the size and flow of this mighty arm of the sea. In French, a different word (*fleuve*) is used to distinguish a great river from a tiny stream (*rivière*); the St. Lawrence certainly deserves this name. Similarly, I find it hard to use the word "lake" for the huge inland seas that are the Great Lakes, each with its own character and magnificent to behold.

Eastern Canada is a land of great variety. Nowhere is this more true than in the Atlantic provinces, where you can experience the Bay of Fundy and its dramatic tides, the wild Atlantic coast of Nova Scotia, spectacular Cape Breton, the tranquil beauty of Prince Edward Island and the rugged landscapes of Newfoundland.

I adore living in Montréal and I relish the occasional conflict of cultures that gives the city such vibrancy. French Canada has all the Gallic charm of the mother country, with fine

Right: *the harbor at Baie-St-Paul*

cuisine and an enviable *joie de vivre*. I also look forward to my visits to Toronto to attend a show or an exhibition in one of its magnificent museums.

Finally, despite the crowds, I cannot imagine a year going by without standing on the brink of Niagara Falls watching all that water endlessly falling over the rock edge.

Eastern Canada's Features

Geography
• Population: just over 23 million.
• Most of Ontario, Québec and Labrador are part of the Canadian Shield, rich in minerals, covered with forest and traversed by fast-flowing rivers.
• The five Great Lakes cover just over 246,031sq km (95,000 square miles). The deepest is Lake Superior, with a maximum depth of 406m (1,332 feet).
• The St. Lawrence River is Eastern Canada's major waterway. Although it is only 1,223km (760 miles) long, its drainage basin covers nearly 518,000sq km (200,000 square miles).
• The highest peak of Eastern Canada is Mount Caubuick (1,652m/5,420 feet) in the Torngat Mountains of Labrador.
• Newfoundland's craggy coastline stretches for around 9,600km (6,000 miles).

Animal Life
• The northern forests are the domain of moose, caribou, deer, beaver and a variety of bears.
• Canada geese can be found all over the region. They are particularly prominent during migration times, when they fly in vast V-shaped formations and are very noisy.
• Snow geese spend a month or more in the St. Lawrence tidal flats near Québec City every spring and fall.

• Point Pelee in Lake Erie is a famous location for birdwatching (and spotting monarch butterflies), especially during the migration periods (▶ 88).
• A variety of whales can be seen in the St. Lawrence near the mouth of the Saguenay every summer, and there is a resident beluga population here too (▶ 26, Top Ten).

Sports and Leisure
• Hockey is the national obsession, and it's played on ice of course!
• Iceskating is universally popular – the winters are long and cold.
• Curling was introduced by the Scots and is practically the national sport.
• The fabulous natural countryside of Eastern Canada is ideal for outdoor activities such as camping and fishing (▶ 12–13).
• An abundance of rivers, lakes and streams makes canoeing a popular pastime (▶ 12–13).
• After the cold winter, the whole country celebrates a multitude of festivals in style all summer long (▶ 116).

Left: *Canada geese*

Below: *fishing on the St. Lawrence River*

7

Essence of Eastern Canada

Eastern Canada is huge, so don't try to see all of it in one go. Instead, include a little of everything when planning your trip. The Atlantic coast is an essential destination, from the unique and intriguing lifestyle of Newfoundland to the wonderful scenery of Cape Breton. Inland are more natural beauties: the vast Great Lakes, rivers ideal for canoeing and the ever-popular Niagara Falls.

Falls colors along the Cabot Trail

Toronto's contemporary skyline – all concrete, steel and glass

Eastern Canada also boasts sophisticated and attractive urban centers. Toronto has impressive modern architecture, Montréal abounds in numerous splendid restaurants, Ottawa offers first-class museums and Québec has a stunning site and a resolutely French face. In all, there's something here for everyone.

THE **10** ESSENTIALS

If you only have a short time to visit Eastern Canada, or would like to get a really complete picture of the region, here are the essentials:

• **Dangle your feet in the water** at the town wharf in St. Andrews-by-the-Sea (➤ 41) and watch the huge tide changes in the Bay of Fundy (➤ 18, Top Ten, and ➤ 36).

• **Take the boat trip** into Western Brook Pond in Gros Morne National Park (➤ 36 and 37) to wonder at this spectacular and deserted fjord.

• **Enjoy a lobster supper** on Prince Edward Island (➤ 40).

• **Picnic on the slopes of the Citadelle** in Québec City (➤ 55) on a summer's evening and watch the sun set across the St. Lawrence River.

• **Order a beer** (or a café au lait, if it's early in the day) at one of the *café-terrasses* on place Jacques Cartier (➤ 51) in Montréal and watch the world walk by.

• **Take a jet-boat trip up the St. Lawrence** to the Lachine Rapids near Montréal and get soaked by the spray (or, for the adventurous, raft down the same rapids).

• **Visit Kensington Market** in Toronto (➤ 77) on a Saturday afternoon to experience the city's amazing ethnic diversity.

• **Go to the top of the CN Tower** (➤ 17, Top Ten) – after all, it is the world's tallest free-standing building!

• **Skate the length of the Rideau Canal** in Ottawa (➤ 73) in February, especially at the end of the day to watch the civil servants skating home from work as the sun sets.

• **Stand on the brink of the Niagara Falls** (➤ 20–21, Top Ten) and be mesmerized by the falling water. You may even forget the crowds!

Below: *street café on Montréal's place Jacques Cartier*

Bottom: *dramatic scenery at Gros Morne National Park*

The Shaping of Eastern Canada

13,000 years ago
Toward the end of the last ice age, the first human beings arrive in North America by land bridge from Siberia, eventually spreading across the continent into eastern Canada.

10th century
Norsemen under the leadership of Leif Ericsson settle briefly near L'Anse aux Meadows, Newfoundland, calling their colony Vinland.

1497
Sailing under an English flag, Italian navigator and cartographer Giovanni Caboto (John Cabot) visits the coast of Newfoundland and writes about the rich fisheries. By this stage, Basque fishermen had already visited the Labrador coast.

1534–35
In search of the Orient, Jacques Cartier explores the Gulf of St. Lawrence and the river as far inland as the future site of Montréal. He claims the land for France.

1583
In the harbor of St. John's, Newfoundland, Sir Humphrey Gilbert claims the land for England.

1604
The first European colony in Canada is established on the coast of Nova Scotia by Frenchmen Samuel de Champlain and the Sieur de Monts. A year later, they found Port Royal (► 34).

1608
French explorer Samuel de Champlain founds Québec City. Over the next few years, he explores a large part of southern Québec and Ontario.

1642
Ville-Marie de Montréal is founded as a Roman Catholic mission by Paul Chomedy de Maisonneuve (► 45).

17th–18th centuries
French explorers and missionaries extend "Nouvelle France" over much of Eastern Canada. There is almost constant war between France and England.

1749
Halifax is founded by the English as a military base to rival the French fortress of Louisbourg in Nova Scotia (► 38).

1756–63
The Seven Years War culminates with a British victory on the Plains of Abraham (► 53). Thereafter, Eastern Canada is British territory.

1774
The Québec Act gives French Canadians the right to preserve their language, religion and civil law.

1775–76
American troops occupy Montréal and are defeated before the walls of Québec.

1783 and after
After the American Revolution, thousands of American Loyalists settle in "British" North America, founding New Brunswick and Ontario.

1793
John Graves Simcoe founds York (now Toronto) in what was then "Upper Canada."

Bust of French explorer and navigator Jacques Cartier (1491–1557)

Gold medal
from the 1976
Montréal Olympics

1812–14
The War of 1812 between the U.S.A. and Britain confirms a separate Canadian identity in North America.

July 1, 1867
Canada officially comes into existence as a confederation of four provinces – Ontario, Québec, Nova Scotia and New Brunswick.

1873
Prince Edward Island joins the Canadian Confederation.

1914–18
Some 650,000 Canadians enlist and 60,000 are killed in World War I.

December 6, 1917
The Halifax Explosion occurs (► 31), the greatest man-made explosion in the world before the atomic bomb is dropped on Hiroshima.

1939–45
During World War II, 1.1 million Canadians serve, 42,042 are killed, and 54,414 are wounded.

1949
Newfoundland and Labrador joins the Canadian Confederation as the tenth province.

1965
Canada adopts the maple leaf flag.

1967
The centenary of Canadian Confederation is celebrated, especially at Expo 67 in Montréal (► 49).

October 1970
Continued terrorist attacks, kidnappings and murders in Québec result in the introduction of the War Measures Act.

1976
The summer Olympic games are held in Montréal.

1980 and 1995
Referendums in Québec confirm the province's desire to remain part of Canada.

1982
The Canadian Constitution is patriated by Pierre Trudeau without Québec's agreement.

2004
Canada is rocked by the misappropriation of millions of dollars put aside to promote the federal government in Québec.

The national flag with its distinctive maple leaf

Peace & Quiet

Eastern Canadians are past masters at getting away from it all. A huge percentage of urban dwellers own or rent a weekend house beside a lake or river within comfortable driving distance of their primary residence. Visitors can also take advantage of this lifestyle and easily rent a cabin in which to enjoy a little peace and quiet.

National Parks

Eastern Canada is blessed with some magnificent national parks where it is easy to follow a trail and leave civilization behind. Gros Morne (► 36 and 37), Cape Breton Highlands (► 39) and Fundy (► 17, Top Ten, and ► 36) are all spectacular, but there are many others that offer less traveled routes, lakes and wilderness campsites. For example, interior Nova Scotia can be appreciated at Kejimkujik, the New Brunswick coast on the Gulf of St. Lawrence can be enjoyed at Kouchibouguac, Québec has a wonderful forest park north of Trois-Rivières called the Mauricie, and Ontario's wild shore on Lake Superior is best seen at Pukaskwa.

Canoeing Country

What could be more Canadian than going canoeing on pristine deserted waters? Renting a canoe is an easy way of getting away from other people and closer to wildlife. Algonquin Provincial Park in Ontario (► 83) comprises a huge network of interconnected lakes and waterways that offer almost 1,600km (1,000 miles) of canoe routes. To the north and west of Lake Superior, Quetico Provincial Park is

Smoke Lake, Algonquin Provincial Park

equally well endowed and even more remote than Algonquin Provincial Park. In northern Québec, Parc Provincial de la Vérendrye is another area renowned for its canoe routes.

Sunsets over Lake Huron

Lake Huron is a very beautiful stretch of water, a gorgeous deep blue color. Watching the sun set across it on a fine evening is particularly magnificent, as are the occasional summer displays of the aurora borealis in the night sky. The Ontario shoreline both north and south of Goderich has some deserted stretches that are ideal for appreciating these phenomena.

Gaspésie

This huge peninsula offers many opportunities for getting away from it all. It has a mountainous center with good hiking in Parc de la Gaspésie, and the rocky coastline can be appreciated in all its wildness in Forillon National Park (▶ 62).

Along the shores of Lake Huron

Labrador

Even the name Labrador conjures up a wild, deserted land, and this is exactly what it is. It may even be a little too wild for some – hiking in the Torngat Mountains in the north of the region, for example, requires advanced survival skills – so you may prefer to stay slightly closer to civilization.

Deserted Beaches

The most beautiful sandy beaches of the region are found on Prince Edward Island. The water here certainly isn't warm, but it's infinitely preferable to the freezing Atlantic swells of the Nova Scotia or Newfoundland coasts. Elsewhere, there are a great many pristine lakes, notably in northern Ontario.

Urban Oases

Even Eastern Canada's cities hide a few retreats for visitors seeking a little peace and quiet. Mont-Royal Park in Montréal is a pleasant oasis above the city and has some wonderful views (▶ 19, Top Ten). In Toronto, there are many parks along the ravines that cross the city, and it's delightful to take the ferry to the Toronto Islands on a weekday (▶ 82) and sit looking at Lake Ontario.

Eastern Canada's Famous

Cirque du Soleil
Another eastern Canadian creation is Guy Laliberté's Cirque du Soleil, which started life in 1984 as a collection of street performers. It has evolved into a fast-moving, almost magical spectacle of lights, movement and music in a category all of its own. There are jugglers, acrobats, contortionists and gymnasts, but absolutely no animal acts. Based in Montréal, as of 2004 it had eight mega productions touring internationally or in residence in Las Vegas and Orlando.

Screen and Stage

The most successful and best-known eastern Canadian film director is French Canadian Denys Arcand, whose movie *Les Invasions Barbères (The Barbarian Invasions)* won an Oscar for best foreign-language production in 2004. Other films by Arcand include *The Decline of the American Empire* and *Jesus of Montréal*. Where musical performances are concerned, Luc Plamondon from Québec City has had phenomenal success, especially with his mega productions *Starmania* and *Notre-Dame de Paris*.

Michel Tremblay is the best-known eastern Canadian playwright at the present time. He revolutionized the theater scene in Québec with his works in *joual* (slang). Tremblay's plays have all been translated into English, and include *Les Belles Soeurs* (in Scottish dialect *The Guid Sisters*), *Albertine in Five Times*, *Forever Yours, Mary-Lou*, and *For the Pleasure of Seeing Her Again*.

Above: *Cirque du Soleil – playing with fire*

Pop Icons and Jazz Greats

Turning to popular music, the fame of two very different women has transcended Canadian borders. Pop diva Céline Dion from Montréal and country music star Shania Twain from Timmins, northern Ontario, are among the highest-selling female recording artists ever, and their popularity has reached phenomenal proportions. Céline Dion sang the title music for the film *Titanic* ("My Heart Will Go On") and has recorded many of Luc Plamondon's songs.

With its free concerts, the Montréal International Jazz festival (▶ 116) is a renowned summer event that has brought such local stars as Oscar Peterson, Charlie Biddle, Renee Lee and Oliver Jones to the limelight.

Literature

The great names of eastern Canadian literature include the late Ontarian novelist Robertson Davies, with works such as *The Deptford Trilogy* and *The Cunning Man*. Montréal Jewish life is vividly brought to life in the books of Mordecai Richler, such as *The Apprenticeship of Duddy Kravitz* and *St. Urbain's Horsemen*. The name of Toronto writer Margaret Atwood has also transcended Canadian borders with triumphs such as *Life Before Man*, *The Handmaid's Tail*, *Alias Grace* and the Booker Prize-winning *The Blind Assassin*.

Above: *country music star Shania Twain*

Right: *jazz pianist and composer Oscar Petersen*

Top Ten

Above: *the brink of the Horseshoe,
Niagara Falls*

1

Canadian Museum of Civilization (Gatineau)

www.civilization.ca

 69F3

✉ 100 Laurier Street, P.O. Box 3100, Station B, Gatineau, Québec, J8X 4H2. The museum is easily accessible from Ottawa (Ontario) by bridge

☎ 819/776-7000, 800/555-5621 (toll-free)

🕐 Daily

🍴 Restaurant ($$$), cafeteria ($)

♿ Very good

✋ Expensive; free Thu 4–9; half-price Sun. Parking charge

↔ Ottawa (➤ 68–73)

❓ Guided tours. Craft boutique, IMAX movie theater, Children's Museum

The Great Hall with its totem poles and cedar log houses

Their curved lines evoking the birth of the North American continent, the buildings of the Canadian Museum of Civilization are stunning, quite the most interesting architectural ensemble in Canada.

The two extraordinary structures that make up the Canadian Museum of Civilization occupy a fine site beside the Ottawa River, directly across from the Canadian Parliament Buildings (➤ 72). The masterpiece of Edmonton architect Douglas Cardinal, opened in 1989, they suggest the emergence of man on a continent sculpted and eroded by wind, water and glacier. Even the Manitoba limestone used as cladding is significant, with its fossils dating from early geological times. The less dramatic of the two structures is the curatorial block. The museum proper is characterized by large glass walls and huge copper vaults and domes – there is more copper here than in any other building in the world.

The majestic Great Hall forms the museum's architectural centerpiece, occupying a whopping 1,782sq m (19,182 square feet) of space and with floor-to-ceiling windows rising 112m (365 feet). It houses six complete cedar log houses of the Pacific coast peoples set along a shoreline with forest backdrop, and includes a magnificent collection of totem poles

A large and complex contemporary sculpture by Bill Reid stands at the far end of the Great Hall. Called *Spirit of Haida Gwaii*, this original plaster shows a Haida canoe full of people paddling vigorously.

Under a vast domed ceiling, the Canada Hall features full-scale buildings in and around which real-life characters bring alive a panorama of Canadian history. Highlights include a Basque whaling station on the Labrador coast, a town square from New France, a bustling shipyard in New Brunswick and an early Loyalist settlement in Ontario.

2
CN Tower
(Toronto)

The ultimate symbol of modern Toronto, this needle-thin mast with a bulge two-thirds the way up is the world's tallest free-standing structure. The view from it is nothing short of spectacular.

The CN Tower rises an incredible 553.33m (1,815 feet 5 inches). Love it or hate it, there's no denying that it has enhanced Toronto's skyline since its construction in the 1970s. Glass-fronted elevators climb to the Look Out, two-thirds of the way up (346m, or 1,136 feet, above the ground) at a stomach-churning speed of 6m (20 feet) a second. The city's landmarks can easily be identified either from inside or from an outdoor observatory one floor down. Those with a good head for heights can even look directly down at the ground through a glass floor.

Don't miss the ascent to the Sky Pod, another 33 floors up, or 447m (1,465 feet) above the ground. This is the highest man-made observatory in the world and the view is superb. You feel as though you are in an airplane, especially when you see real planes landing at Toronto Islands Airport below you. Visibility can exceed 160km (100 miles) and, with luck, you will be able to make out the spray of Niagara Falls and the city of Rochester, New York state, across Lake Ontario. You should be aware, however, that the tower can sway up to 1.8m (6 feet) from the vertical on windy days – a normal but somewhat unnerving sensation.

The CN Tower was not primarily intended as a tourist attraction, but was built as a telecommunications tower. In the 1960s, Toronto experienced a construction boom that transformed the skyline from one characterized by relatively low buildings into one dotted with skyscrapers. These new buildings caused serious communications problems as they got in the way of the airwaves. The CN Tower, with microwave receptors at 338m (1,109 feet) and topped by an antenna, effectively solved these difficulties.

www.cntower.ca

✠ 69E2

✉ 301 Front Street, Toronto, Ontario, M5V 2T6

☎ 416/868-6937

🕐 Daily; closed Dec 25; hours of operation adjusted seasonally

🍴 Restaurant ($$$)

🚇 Union

♿ Very good

✋ Very expensive

↔ SkyDome (► 79); Harbourfront Centre (► 75)

❓ Souvenir shops. Long lines during peak times and seasons

The CN Tower has a revolving restaurant 351m (1,151 feet) above ground

3
Hopewell Rocks
(Bay of Fundy)

www.thehopewellrocks.ca

✚ 44C2

🍴 Food service ($), picnic area

♿ Few

✋ Parking: moderate

↔ Fundy National Park (► 36)

❓ Morning light is best for photography. Located 40km (25 miles) south of Moncton on Route 114

Hopewell Rocks Interpretive Centre

✉ 131 Discovery Road, Hopewell Cape, New Brunswick, E4H 4Z5

☎ 506/734-3534, 877/734-3429 (toll-free in Canada)

🕐 Daily, mid-May to mid-Oct

Hopewell Cape's strange but beautiful sea-sculpted rocks

Slender rock "flowerpots" that tower up to 15m (50 feet) above the sand at low tide become tiny tree-covered islets when the tide is fully risen.

Overlooking Shepody Bay of the Bay of Fundy, Hopewell Cape experiences a difference of nearly 10m (33 feet) between high and low tides. This tidal action has cut rock formations out of the high sandstone cliffs that are known as "flowerpots," because their narrow bases widen to support dwarf fir and spruce trees on the top.

The enormous tidal ranges found in the Bay of Fundy are the result of an unusual combination of factors. Like water in a bathtub, the water in the bay has a natural rocking motion called a seiche. The Atlantic Ocean tide that floods into the bay every 12 hours and 25 minutes increases this rocking motion, and in addition water is forced higher up the shores of the bay as it becomes narrower and shallower towards its head. Consequently, the tide at the bay's northern end can rise and fall up to an incredible 16m (52 feet), a phenomenon that can be appreciated in a number of places but none more so than Hopewell Cape.

At low tide, you can descend a steep staircase and walk out onto the sand around the rocks. At high tide, you can't even reach the bottom of the stairs, so make sure you check the status of the tide before you take a beach walk. Not only is the difference between high and low tides very large, but the tide comes in fast – between 1.8 and 2.4m (6–8 feet) per hour. There is a tide timetable posted at the Interpretive Center, which also has displays explaining the whole phenomenon.

4
Mont-Royal
Chalet (Montréal)

Mont-Royal Park, the jewel in Montréal's crown, was created by the landscape architect Frederick Law Olmstead, and offers magnificent views of the city and river from its Chalet viewpoint.

At the center of the island of Montréal and deep in the heart of the city, the bulky lump of Mont-Royal rises 228m (750 feet). "La Montagne" (the Mountain) is not only a lovely park, but it is also part of the city's soul. It provides a wonderful oasis of greenery in the center of the densely populated and bustling metropolis, and as such is popular with residents year-round and very precious to them.

In 1876, the city expropriated the land at the top of the mountain for a hefty Can$1 million, and then invited Frederick Law Olmstead (famous for designing Central Park in New York) to landscape it. Near the summit, the large stone Chalet was built between 1931 and 1932 as a reception center.

High above the bustle of the city, the Chalet offers views that are nothing less than spectacular. The downtown highrises are particularly prominent – look for the distinctive greystone buildings of the McGill University campus, topped with their green copper roofs. The mighty St. Lawrence can be seen winding its way around the city, and on clear days the Adirondack Mountains of northern New York state are visible, as are the Green Mountains of Vermont. The view is equally spectacular at night, and in the winter months the cold gives it an additional clarity.

The wide, flat St. Lawrence valley is punctuated by a series of small, rather dramatic peaks like Mont-Royal, which were created about 60 million years ago during a period of tectonic activity. These igneous plugs are known as the Collines Montérégiennes (Monteregian Hills), from *mons regius*, the Latin name for Mont-Royal. According to most historians, the city's name also derives from Mont-Royal. In 1535, the French explorer Jacques Cartier climbed to the top of the peak and is said to have exclaimed "It's a royal mountain" when he saw the view.

www.lemontroyal.qc.ca

✚ 44A1

✉ Parc du Mont-Royal, Voie Camillien-Houde, Montréal, Québec

☎ 514/843-8240

🕐 Daily

🍴 Cafeteria ($) at Chalet

🚌 11 from Mont-Royal métro station

♿ Good from parking lot

✋ Free. Parking charge

↔ Montréal (➤ 45–51)

❓ Accessible on foot from rue Peel at avenue des Pins (200 steps; allow 20 minutes)

The spectacular view from Mont-Royal Park

5
Niagara Falls

www.niagaraparks.com

✚ 69E2

✉ Niagara Parks Commission, 7400 Portage Road South, P.O. Box 150, Oak Hall Administrative Building, Niagara Falls, Ontario, L2E 6T2

☎ 905/371-0254, 877/642-7275

🍴 Huge variety of restaurants and cafés

🚌 People Mover bus: daily, Mar–Dec

⛴ *Maid of the Mist*: daily, late Apr–Oct

♿ Good

✋ Parking: expensive. Boat tour: expensive

↔ Niagara-on-the-Lake (▶ 85); Niagara Parkway (▶ 85 and 87)

In 1678, French explorer Louis Hennepin exclaimed, "The universe does not afford its parallel," a sentiment still echoed by the millions of people who flock to Niagara Falls every year.

Is there anyone who has not heard of Niagara? This famous waterfall is one of the best-known, most visited and most photographed sights in the entire world. Around 14 million people visit it annually, taking an estimated 100 million photographs. The fascination of watching all that "thundering water" (the meaning of the First Nations word Niagara) endlessly flowing over the rock edge has a totally mesmerizing effect on everyone who sees it. Few are disappointed; many are more impressed than they expected to be. Niagara Falls are quite simply fantastic.

Just before it reaches tiny Goat Island, the Niagara River divides into two. About 10 percent of the water

Inset: *the Falls illuminated at night*

heads for the American Falls (so called because they are on the U.S. side of the river), which are more than 300m (985 feet) wide and 54m (176 feet) high. Ninety percent of the water heads for the Canadian, or Horseshoe Falls, which are named for their shape and are nearly 800m (2,625 feet) wide and about 51m (167 feet) high. The water crashes over the falls at the incredible rate of 155 million liters (40 million gallons) per minute.

At Table Rock, you can approach the very edge of the Horseshoe Falls, the point where the tumultuous water plunges over the cliff. It is incredibly impressive, but it can also be wet on windy days. From here you can descend by elevator to two outdoor observation decks directly behind the falls – also impressive and wet. And nobody should miss the exciting (and wet) *Maid of the Mist* boat ride, which goes right into the middle of the horseshoe.

Approaching Horseshoe Falls aboard the Maid of the Mist *(above). Disposable waterproofs are provided (left)*

6
Rocher Percé
(Gaspésie)

www.rocherperce.com

✚ 29A2

🍴 Variety of restaurants
and cafés in Percé

ℹ Information touristique
de Percé: 142 Route
132, P.O. Box 99,
Percé, Québec, G0C
2L0 ☎ 418/782-5448

♿ Few

↔ Gaspésie (► 62)

❓ Boat tours in summer
only (details available
from tourist information
office)

*A massive pierced limestone rock sits seemingly at
anchor just off the tiny community of Percé at the
end of the magnificent Gaspé Peninsula.*

Rocher Percé is a limestone block formed from layers of
sediment deposited on the seabed about 375 million years
ago. It soars high above the surrounding sand to 88m (289
feet) and is an amazing 438m (1,437 feet) in length. At its
eastern end, it is pierced by an arch. Once there were two
arches here, but in 1848, during a storm, one collapsed to
leave the separate pinnacle now known as the Obelisk.

Renowned for the beauty of its site, the village of Percé
is blessed with a varied topography, and nowhere else on
the peninsula are the geological forces that shaped
Gaspésie more evident. Yellowish limestone and red
conglomerate rock have been pushed, squeezed and
folded into protruding cliffs, deep bays and craggy hills.

You can park in the town and walk out to Rocher Percé
– or even around it if the tide is out. Every cape and
headland in the community offers a different view. Mont-
Ste.-Anne, the craggy peak dominating the town, has
particularly splendid panoramas, although the path leading
up it is steep (the trail begins beside the church; allow 1.5
hours to reach the summit). You get another wonderful
view of Rocher Percé by taking the boat tour to
Bonaventure Island, which passes close to the rock before
making a circular tour of the island famous for its seabirds,
notably its huge gannet colony.

*The Rocher Percé as
seen from the boat tour
to Bonaventure Island*

7

Science North (Sudbury)

Set in an oval crater in the Precambrian Canadian Shield, this is a stunning science center hewn out of the rock below two glittering snowflake-shaped buildings.

www.sciencenorth.on.ca

✚ 69D3

✉ 100 Ramsey Lake Road, Sudbury, Ontario, P3E 5S9

☎ 705/522-3701, 800/461-4898 (toll-free), 705/522-3700 (recorded message)

🕐 Daily

🍴 Restaurant ($$), cafeteria ($)

🚢 Boat cruises on Ramsey Lake

♿ Good

✋ Expensive

↔ Sudbury (▶ 89)

❓ Whizards Gift Store

Even if you find science the most boring thing on Earth, you will be impressed by Science North, in Sudbury, deep in northern Ontario's mining belt. The two unusual snowflake buildings, representing the glaciation that sculpted the Canadian landscape, opened in 1984 and are nothing short of amazing in this nickel-mining industrial city. Raymond Moriyama was the architect, and he clad the exterior of the snowflakes in stainless steel, the main ingredient of which is the nickel mined locally.

The smaller snowflake houses the reception area, while the larger snowflake, about 60m (200 feet) away, contains the exhibits. An underground rock tunnel links the two buildings, ending in a huge underground cavern representing the crater in which Sudbury sits and used as a theater for a spectacular 3-D movie. From the cavern, visitors proceed to the exhibit floors along a glass-enclosed ramp that offers views of Ramsey Lake and part of a fault that runs through the rock at this point. This rock fault was deliberately excavated for its geological interest.

As far as the exhibits are concerned, you have to roll up your sleeves and get involved. You can have a go at building and programming a robot in the LEGO Mindstorms Robotics Lab, and if that doesn't appeal, you can hold a snake or watch beavers or flying squirrels in action. There are also laser shows and IMAX movies; the Virtual Voyages Adventure Ride, which combines motion simulator technology with high-resolution animation on a huge screen; and a tropical greenhouse where 400 tropical butterflies fly free.

Try your hand at operating a Canadarm on the space shuttle

23

8
Signal Hill
(St. John's)

www.parkscanada.gc.ca

 29C3

 P.O. Box 1268, St. John's, Newfoundland and Labrador, A1C 5M9

 709/772-5367

 Daily. Visitor center: daily 8:30–8, mid-Jun to Labour day; Mon–Fri 8:30–4:30, mid-Oct to mid-May; daily 8:30–4:30, rest of year

 Picnic facilities

Few

Signal Hill: free. Visitor center: inexpensive

 Avalon Peninsula (► 34)

 Military drills are performed by cadets Jul–Aug. Gift shop in Cabot Tower

Below: *authentically dressed soldier at old Quidi Vidi Battery*

The Newfoundland capital has a spectacular site on the slopes of a natural harbor whose narrow entrance is guarded by the great rock of Signal Hill.

No visit to St. John's would be complete without a climb up Signal Hill for panoramic views of the city, harbor and coastline. A calm day is best for the excursion – if there is even a light breeze in the city, the wind will be strong on Signal Hill. The cliffs rise sharply to form this rocky and barren outcrop facing the Atlantic Ocean. At the top stands Cabot Tower, the city's best-known landmark, built in 1897 to commemorate the 400th anniversary of John Cabot's visit to Newfoundland. From here, you can look straight down into The Narrows, the 200m wide (650-foot) entrance to the harbor, while to the southeast is Cape Spear, North America's most easterly point.

As its name suggests, Signal Hill has long been used for signalling. From the early 18th century, flags were flown from its summit to alert local merchants to the approach of their vessels. In 1901, a different type of communication took place when Guglielmo Marconi received the first transatlantic wireless signal from Poldhu in Cornwall, England. That letter "s" in Morse code traversed more than 2,700km (1,700 miles) to make history, an event commemorated by a communications display in Cabot Tower.

Right: *old cannon at the Queen's Battery and view of the city*

Today a national historic park, Signal Hill has a visitor center and a great trail system. From Cabot Tower, you can walk over to Queen's Battery or to Ladies Lookout at 160m (525 feet), while other trails lead to such wonderfully named places as Quidi Vidi, Cuckolds Cove and Gibbet Hill. Avid hikers can descend the North Head to The Narrows via a steep trail on the ocean side.

9

Terrasse Dufferin & Promenade des Gouverneurs (Québec City)

Admiring the city from the Dufferin Terrace and then following the spectacular Governors' Walk as it clings to the cliff face is one of the glories of a visit to Québec.

The Terrasse Dufferin (Dufferin Terrace) is a wide wooden boardwalk suspended high above the St. Lawrence River, offering magnificent views over the surrounding country. Extending for a total of 670m (2,200 feet), it is popular year-round, day and night. On summer evenings, there are performing musicians, and lovers stroll by hand in hand. In the winter, you can try the toboggan slide or watch the tourists slipping about on the ice as they take photographs.

The history of Terrasse Dufferin starts in 1620 with Samuel de Champlain, whose statue stands on the terrace in front of the Château Frontenac. He constructed the Château St. Louis here, which served as the residence of first the French, and later the British, governors until it was destroyed by fire in 1834. At that time, the British governor, Lord Durham, built a platform over the ruins and allowed public access. The structure was then extended on a couple of occasions, notably in 1879 by Governor General Lord Dufferin, whose name it commemorates.

From the terrace's southern end, and accessed by a steep flight of stairs, a spectacular boardwalk inaugurated in 1960 clings to the cliff about 90m (300 feet) above the river. This is the Promenade des Gouverneurs (Governors' Walk), which goes around the outer walls of the Citadelle (▶ 55) with splendid views of the St. Lawrence, the Basse-Ville (Lower Town), Île d'Orléans and the opposite shore of the river as far as the mountains of northern Maine on a clear day. If you don't mind climbing its 310 steps, it provides an excellent means of getting to the Plains of Abraham; alternatively, it offers a magnificent way of arriving in Québec if you descend it from the Plains of Abraham (allow 20 minutes one way).

✚ 44B2

🕐 Terrasse Dufferin: daily. Promenade des Gouverneurs: daily, May–Oct

🍴 Restaurants and cafés nearby

♿ Terrasse Dufferin: good. Promenade des Gouverneurs: none

✋ Free

↔ Québec City (▶ 53–57, 60)

❓ Terrasse Dufferin adjoins place d'Armes in front of Château Frontenac. Promenade des Gouverneurs runs from the southern end of Terrasse Dufferin to avenue du Cap-Diamant in National Battlefields Park

Château Frontenac

10
Whale-watching (Tadoussac)

The rich waters at the point where the Saguenay River joins the St. Lawrence have long attracted giant mammals of the deep, and have made Tadoussac a famous whale-watching center.

🕇 44B2

🍴 Variety of restaurants in Tadoussac

♿ Limited

✋ Very expensive

↔ Saguenay Fjord (► 65)

❓ Aug is considered the best month for spotting whales

Croisières AML
www.croisieresaml.com

✉ 124 rue St-Pierre, Québec City, Québec, G1K 4A7

☎ 418/692-2634, 800/563-4643 (toll-free)

🕐 Daily, Jul–early Sep

Famille Dufour Croisières
www.groupedufour.com

✉ 22 quai St.-André, Québec City, Québec, G1K 7B9

☎ 418/692-0222, 800/463-5250 (toll-free)

🕐 Daily, Jun–Sep

Whale-watching is a highlight of any trip

Every day, the salty tides of the St. Lawrence River sweep into the mouth of the Saguenay, and in its turn the main stream is invaded by the fresh waters of its tributary. This mixture of waters has created a rich ecosystem where plankton flourishes. Small creatures such as krill, shrimp and capelin feed on this plankton, attracting in their turn larger predators. A resident population of about 500 beluga, or white whales, haunts these waters, and they are joined in June by numerous other species. Fin and minke whales are frequently viewed off Tadoussac, and occasionally humpback whales are sighted. Some people have even glimpsed the great blue whale, the biggest mammal on Earth, growing to as much as 30m (100 feet) in length and weighing up to 100 tonnes (2,200 pounds).

Tadoussac has a fine site on the cliffs and sand dunes along the north shore of the St. Lawrence, but it is rare to spot whales from the shore. The St. Lawrence is more than 10km (6 miles) wide at this point, and it is mid-river, miles from shore, that the whales frolic, rising above the water to breathe and diving to search for food. Great jets of water issue from their blowholes just before they surface, so they are fairly easy to spot.

Throughout the summer months, a procession of small boats leaves Tadoussac wharf, offering a variety of tours of varying lengths. The views of the town and the mouth of the Saguenay are magnificent. Standing on a shoal close to the junction of these two important waterways is the Prince Light, a 15m-high (50-foot) lighthouse that was constructed after the Prince of Wales' ship ran aground here in the 1880s.

What To See

Above: *Neil's Harbour, Cape Breton*
Right: *statue of the Virgin Mary atop the Chapelle Notre-Dame de Bonsecours*

Atlantic Provinces

At the extreme eastern edge of Canada lie the provinces of New Brunswick, Nova Scotia, Prince Edward Island, and Newfoundland and Labrador. Steeped in the spray of the Atlantic Ocean, they are the smallest of all the Canadian provinces in both size and population. They are nevertheless strong in their traditional heritage, reflecting French Acadian roots, the earliest Loyalist settlements, the Gaelic culture of the Highland Scots and, in the case of Newfoundland, a strong Irish legacy. They boast major cities such as Halifax and St. John's, charming communities like Charlottetown, Fredericton, St. Andrews-by-the-Sea, Lunenburg and Annapolis Royal, and the major historical restorations of Louisbourg and Village Historique Acadien. The scenery is amazingly varied, from the dramatic fjords of Gros Morne and the impressive seascapes of mountainous Cape Breton to the pretty rural landscape of Prince Edward Island and the fabulous tides of the Bay of Fundy.

'Here is material rich and unwrought waiting for pen — landscape, legend, and tradition; ... the great tides, the wide marshes, the vast red gaping channels, supply subjects which are new both in line and colour; and the moisture in the bland air gives 'atmosphere' to soften all harsh edges.'

CHARLES G. D. ROBERTS
The Canadian Guide-Book: The Tourist's and Sportsman's Guide to Eastern Canada and Newfoundland (1892)

ATLANTIC PROVINCES

0   200 km
0   150 miles

Cartwright

Battle Harbour

NEWFOUNDLAND

Red Bay   St Anthony

Lake Melville

North West River

Labrador

Happy Valley-Goose Bay

Blanc Sablon   Englee

Musgrave Harbour

Bonavista Bay   Bonavista

La Scie   Bonavista Peninsula

Mutton Bay

806   Botwood   Gambo   Terra Nova National Park

Gros Morne Mt   Springdale   Gander   Clarenville   Arnold's Cove   Wabana

ST JOHN'S

Churchill   Mealy Mts

550   Petit Mécatina   Long Range Mts   Grand Falls-Windsor   Avalon Peninsula   Conception Bay South

Gros Morne National Park   Deer Lake   Bay Du Nord Wilderness Reserve   Placentia   St Marys

Romaine   Island of Newfoundland

QUÉBEC   Harve-Saint-Pierre   Corner Brook   Harbour Breton   Cape St Mary's

Natashquan   Stephenville Crossing   Marystown

Rivière-au-Tonnerre   Détroit de J. Cartier   St George's Bay   Burgeo   Grand Bank   St-Pierre

Rivière-St-Jean   Île d'Anticosti   Miquelon   (F)

Moisie   Sept-Îles   Détroit d'Honguedo   Channel-Port aux Basques

Port-Cartier   *St Lawrence*   Grande-Vallée   Gulf of St Lawrence   Cabot Strait

Ste-Anne-des-Monts   132   Murdochville   Gaspé   Cap-des-Rosiers   Îles de la Madeleine   Pleasant Bay   Cape Breton Highlands National Park

Matane   Parc de la Gaspésie   Percé   Cap-aux-Meules   Chéticamp   **Sydney**

Mont-Joli   Grande-Rivière   Baddeck   Louisbourg

Carleton   Bonaventure   Bras d'Or Lake   Cape Breton Island

Dalhousie   Caraquet   **Village Historique Acadien**   **PRINCE EDWARD ISLAND**   Souris   Port-Hawkesbury

Rimouski   Bathurst   8   Kensington   **Charlottetown**   Antigonish

St-Quentin   Richibucto   Summerside   New Glasgow

St-Fabien   Ste-Anne-de-Madawaska   108   **NEW BRUNSWICK**   Port Elgin   Truro   **NOVA SCOTIA**

Edmundston   Plaster Rock   **Moncton**   Parrsboro

Hopewell Rocks   Windsor

Fredericton   Sussex   **Fundy National Park**   **HALIFAX**

Woodstock   Middleton   Lunenburg

Saint John   Bay of Fundy   Annapolis Royal

MAINE   McAdam   Fundy Islands   Digby   Liverpool

(USA)   St Andrew by-the-Sea   Argyle   Shelburne

St-Gédéon   Yarmouth

Lac-Mégantic

NH   A   B   C

www.halifaxinfo.com

🔲 29B1

Nova Scotia Visitors Centre

ℹ️ 1595 Barrington Street,
Halifax, Nova Scotia.
Postal address: P.O. Box
456, Halifax, Nova Scotia,
B3J 2R5

☎ 902/424-4248

🕐 Daily

Halifax ✪✪✪

Everything in Halifax is marked by the sea. The waterfront is colorful, with a public walkway stretching for miles, while the city's restaurants, museums and streets are imbued with the ever-present salty feel and smell of the ocean.

Capital of Nova Scotia and the largest city of Atlantic Canada, Halifax is blessed with a magnificent natural harbor that extends nearly 16km (10 miles) inland. The outer harbor is divided from the Bedford Basin by a stretch called The Narrows, where the city climbs up a hill topped by a massive star-shaped fortress. The Citadel continues to dominate the town despite recent highrise construction.

Founded in July 1749, Halifax was from the start a military stronghold and naval base. During World War I, an event

Above: *Queen Victoria's father presented Halifax with the Town Clock in 1803*

Right: *the city's water-front area has a walk that stretches 4km (2.5 miles)*

occurred that left a terrible mark on the city. In 1917, a French munitions ship, the *Mont Blanc*, had a fatal collision with a Belgian relief ship, the *Imo*, in The Narrows. What followed constituted the greatest man-made explosion the world had seen until the dropping of the atom bomb on Hiroshima in 1945. Not only was a huge area of the city destroyed and a large percentage of the population killed or injured, but even today it's impossible to visit the city without finding some reference to this tragedy.

Halifax sits on the second largest natural harbor in the world, after Sydney, Australia

Today, Halifax remains a naval place, home base for the Canadian Navy's Atlantic fleet, and is also an important commercial port with huge container terminals. Although the city sometimes suffers from fog and strong winds off the Atlantic, it is a fascinating place to visit – especially when the sun shines.

What to See in Halifax

ART GALLERY OF NOVA SCOTIA

Located in the heart of the city across the street from the Nova Scotia Legislature, this art gallery occupies two 19th-century buildings connected by the Ondaatje Sculpture Court. The collection is made up of mainly Canadian works, notably some splendid folk art that is displayed creatively. A highlight is part of a house that once belonged to Maud Lewis, an artist from Digby, Nova Scotia, who decorated her home with colorful naive art.

CITADEL

Rising above the city, Citadel Hill offers fine views of its splendid harbor and the two bridges that span The Narrows to connect Halifax with Dartmouth on the opposite shore. Immediately below you is the Town Clock, a gift to the community from Prince Edward, Duke of Kent and father of Queen Victoria. The present Citadel, completed in 1865, is today a national historic site. As you cross the drawbridge, you will meet members of the 78th Highland Regiment, who were stationed here at that time. Wearing MacKenzie tartan kilts, feather bonnets and bright red doublets, they will show you their barracks, guardroom, garrison cell and powder magazine. Each day they fire the noon gun, by which everyone in Halifax sets their clocks – and yes, everyone can hear it, so don't stand too close! An audiovisual presentation, called "Tides of History," makes an excellent introduction to the city.

www.agns.gov.ns.ca
29B1
1723 Hollis Street
902/424-7542
Tue–Sun
Restaurant ($$)
Good
Moderate

www.parkscanada.gc.ca
29B1
P.O. Box 9080, Station A, Halifax, Nova Scotia, B3K 5M7
902/426-5080
Site: daily. Animation: daily, Jun 1–Sep 15
Coffee shop ($)
Few
Expensive Jun–Sep; free rest of year
Regimental gift store. Military drills

The star-shaped Citadel dominates Halifax and its harbor

"Train Station in Winter" by Maud Lewis, Art Gallery of Nova Scotia

HISTORIC PROPERTIES ⊕⊕

In the 1970s, a number of 19th-century warehouses were renovated along the waterfront of Halifax. Today, they house an interesting collection of craft stores and restaurants known as Historic Properties. An excellent food market offers fresh fish and seafood to eat in or take out, as well as a variety of breads, coffees and other edibles.

From Historic Properties, you can walk along the waterfront walkway for a total of 4km (2.5 miles) past the Maritime Museum of the Atlantic, the *Bluenose II* (if she is visiting; ➤ 40, Lunenburg), the ferry to Dartmouth and all kinds of other marine activities. Beyond the new condominium complexes built on the waterfront is **Pier 21**. This national historic site was the entry point to Canada for over a million immigrants between 1928 and 1971, and hence is a popular place of pilgrimage.

MARITIME MUSEUM OF THE ATLANTIC ⊕⊕

With Halifax's history, you would expect it to have an excellent maritime museum, and this one will not disappoint. On the waterfront, partly located in the former William Robertson ship's chandlery, it boasts a number of full-size ships floating beside it as well as an interesting collection of models inside. There is a fascinating display and film on the Halifax Explosion (➤ 31), also displays on the sinking of the *Titanic* in 1912 (150 mostly unidentified bodies found after the disaster were buried in Halifax). There is a section devoted to the Cunard Steamship Line, because Samuel Cunard, its founder, was from Halifax. The highlight is probably the restored ship's chandlery of 1879, complete with owner William Robertson behind the counter.

Outside, during the summer months, you can go on board the HMCS *Sackville*, the sole survivor of more than 100 corvettes that were built in Canada to escort convoys across the Atlantic during World War II. This small but fast armored ship serves as a tribute to all who served in the Canadian Navy during the two world wars.

Historic Properties
✠ 29B1
✉ Access from Lower Water Street
☎ 902/429-0530
🍴 Food market and variety of restaurants ($–$$)
♿ Good
💷 Free. Parking: expensive

Pier 21 National Historic Site
www.pier21.ca
✉ 1055 Marginal Road
☎ 902/425-7770
🕐 Daily, May–Oct; Wed–Sun, rest of year
🍴 Café ($) ♿ Good
💷 Expensive

www.maritime.museum.gov.ns.ca
✠ 29B1
✉ 1675 Lower Water Street
☎ 902/424-7490
🕐 Daily, Jun–Sep, May and Oct; Mon–Sat, Nov–Apr. HMCS *Sackville*: daily, Jun–Sep
🍴 Restaurants nearby ($–$$)
♿ Good
💷 Moderate; small additional fee for HMCS *Sackville*
❓ Gift store with maritime items

www.annapolisroyal.com

🔲 29B1

✉ 285 St. George Street, Annapolis Royal, Nova Scotia ☎ 902/532-2043

Port Royal and Fort Anne National Historic Sites
www.parkscanada.gc.ca

✉ P.O. Box 9, Annapolis Royal, Nova Scotia, B0S 1A0

☎ 902/532-2321

🕐 Daily, mid-May to mid-Oct

🍴 Restaurants in Annapolis Royal ($–$$)

♿ Few 👜 Moderate

🔲 29C3

❓ Witless Bay is 31km (19 miles) south of St. John's via Route 10. Cape St. Mary's is 102km (63 miles) south of the Trans-Canada Highway via Route 100. St. Vincent's is 80km (50 miles) south of the Trans-Canada Highway via Route 90

Cape Spear National Historic Site
www.parkscanada.gc.ca

✉ P.O. Box 1268, St. John's, Newfoundland and Labrador, A1C 5M9

☎ 709/772-5367

🕐 Grounds: daily. Visitor center and lighthouse: daily, mid-May to mid-Oct

🍴 Restaurants in St. John's (▶ 93)

♿ Few 👜 Moderate

↔ St. John's (▶ 24, Top Ten, and 41)

❓ 11km (7 miles) from St. John's via Route 11

The Avalon Peninsula – Canada's "Far East"

What to See in the Atlantic Provinces

ANNAPOLIS ROYAL

Twice daily, the great tides of the Bay of Fundy rush into the Annapolis Basin, reversing the flow of the river at tiny Annapolis Royal. Today, the town is a gracious mixture of heritage and charm, with elegant homes, craft stores and restaurants. Once, however, it was the most fought over place in Canada, changing hands frequently between the English and the French. In the center of the community is **Fort Anne**, whose picturesque site offers sweeping views of the Annapolis Basin from its well-preserved earthworks. A short drive 10.5km (6.5 miles) west takes you to **Port Royal**, founded in 1605 by Samuel de Champlain, making it the first French colony on the continent. The reconstructed wooden buildings, with their steeply pitched roofs and fieldstone chimneys, form a distinctive compound and contain both working and living areas.

AVALON PENINSULA ⭐⭐

On the east coast of Newfoundland, the Avalon Peninsula seems to hang suspended from the rest of the island by a narrow isthmus. At longitude 52° 37' 24" and latitude 47° 31' 17", **Cape Spear** (southeast of St. John's) is the most easterly point of the entire North American continent. Today, it is a national historic park and the lighthouse can be visited. Elsewhere along the peninsula, the coastline is ruggedly beautiful and the wonders of nature are never far away. At St. Vincent's, the water near the beach is deep, so whales come close to shore. Bird Rock, off Cape St. Mary's, has colonies of northern gannets, razorbills and murres, while at Witless Bay, huge icebergs can be seen in early summer, along with more whales and seabirds.

BONAVISTA PENINSULA ★★

On Newfoundland's east coast is the Bonavista Peninsula, which is dotted with a number of picturesque communities. The tiny coastal village of Trinity was once a prosperous fishing center, and although those days have passed, a lot of charm remains. Colorful Newfoundland "box" houses are set on a hilly peninsula that has fine views of the ocean and the small protected harbor. Bonavista is another tranquil community, best known for its rocky cape where John Cabot is supposed to have made his first North American landfall. Cape Bonavista is superb, with pounding waves, a statue of the great explorer and a red and white lighthouse.

CAMPOBELLO ISLAND ★★

Set at the point where the Atlantic Ocean floods into the Bay of Fundy, Campobello Island has long been famous for its invigorating climate. In the late 19th century, wealthy industrialists began building summer homes here, among them the parents of Franklin Delano Roosevelt, U.S. president in 1933–45. Roosevelt and his wife had their own summer "cottage" on the island, which is today the centerpiece of an **international peace park**. Simply furnished, it is a poignant return in time, full of reminders of the lives of its famous former owners.

CAPE BRETON HIGHLANDS NATIONAL PARK (▶ 39)

FREDERICTON ★★

New Brunswick's capital is a quiet, pretty city of elm-lined streets and elegant homes set on a wide bend of the St. John River. It boasts an excellent **art gallery**, the gift of Lord Beaverbrook (he was raised in New Brunswick), with an outstanding collection of British paintings. About 34km (21 miles) west of the city is Kings Landing historical settlement, a fascinating re-creation of 19th-century Loyalist life on a fine site in the St. John valley.

🔡 29C3
🍴 Restaurants in Trinity and Bonavista ($–$$)
❓ Trinity is 74km (46 miles) and Bonavista is 114km (71 miles) from the Trans-Canada Highway at Clarenville via Route 230. Cape Bonavista is 5km (3 miles) from Bonavista.

Above: the Bonavista Peninsula

www.campobello.com
🔡 29A1
ℹ️ Campobello Island Visitor Center ☎ 506/752-7043

Roosevelt-Campobello International Park
www.fdr.net
✉️ 459 Route 774, Campobello Island
☎ 506/752-2922
🕐 Daily, mid-May to mid-Oct
♿ Good
💲 Free (donation requested)

www.city.fredericton.nb.ca
🔡 29A1
✉️ 11 Carleton Street
☎ 506/460-2041

Beaverbrook Art Gallery
✉️ 703 Queen Street
🕐 Daily, mid-May–mid-Oct; Tue–Sun, rest of year

35

www.grandmanannb.com
www.deerisland.nb.ca
🔲 29A1
ℹ️ Grand Manan Tourist
Association and Chamber
of Commerce
☎ 506/662-3442
🚢 Deer Island ferry daily
from Letete, New
Brunswick; Grand Manan
ferry daily from Blacks
Harbour, New Brunswick

www.parkscanada.gc.ca
🔲 29B1
✉️ P.O. Box 1001, Alma,
New Brunswick, E4H 1B4
☎ 506/887-6000
🕐 Daily
🍴 Restaurants, Alma ($–$$)
♿ Few
👋 Free Oct–May; moderate
rest of year

www.
parkscanada.gc.ca/grosmorne
🔲 29B3
✉️ P.O. Box 130, Rocky
Harbour, Newfoundland
and Labrador, A0K 4N0
☎ 709/458-2417
🕐 Daily
🍴 Food services in Rocky
Harbour and Woody Point
($–$$)
♿ Good
👋 Free Oct–May; moderate
rest of year

*Lobster Cove Head
Lighthouse, Gros Morne*

FUNDY ISLANDS

Deer, Grand Manan and Campobello (► 35) islands are located in the mouth of Passamaquoddy Bay, geographically closer to Maine, U.S.A. than to Canada. The high tides, whirlpools and swirling currents of the bay act as giant nutrient pumps, bringing in a mixture of tiny marine organisms that lures all kinds of other creatures, from herring, mackerel and tuna to whales. People visit the islands for a quiet retreat, to watch birds, to view whales and, in the case of Grand Manan, to try dulse, an edible seaweed.

FUNDY NATIONAL PARK

Situated on the Bay of Fundy, this park is a wonderful combination of coastal highlands and shoreline. The bay, with its vast tidal range and cold water, influences the entire park (for details on Fundy tides, ► 18, Top Ten).You can experience this tidal fluctuation on the bay's shores by watching fishing boats come and go. At Alma, it takes less than an hour for the water to go from nothing to waist-deep and the wide beach disappears at high tide.

GROS MORNE NATIONAL PARK

On Newfoundland's west coast is Gros Morne, a spectacularly wild area of fjords, sea coast, forest and mountains. In 1987 it was designated a World Heritage Site by UNESCO for the international importance of its geological features. Preserved in its rocks are indications of vast movements of the Earth's crust and clues to the geological evolution of our planet. The Gros Morne Tablelands consist of peridotite from the Earth's mantle, formed far below the ocean floor and transported hundreds of kilometers to their present position some 450 million years ago. These ocher-colored rocks are an incredibly rare occurrence at the Earth's surface. A visit to the Park Discovery Centre in Woody Point, overlooking beautiful Bonne Bay, offers an excellent introduction. Another spectacular thing to take is the boat trip into Western Brook Pond (► opposite).

A Walk & Boat Trip to Western Brook Pond

Although in Newfoundland a rose may be a rose, a "pond" is almost certainly something else. Western Brook Pond, in Gros Morne National Park, is 16.5km (10 miles) long and is bordered by sheer cliffs that rise 670m (2,200 feet) above its black waters. This oligotrophic (nutrient-poor) lake resembles a fjord and can only properly be appreciated by a walk to its shore and a boat trip along its length.

From the parking area, follow the well–used trail inland toward the great cliffs.

After 1km (0.6 mile), the trail crosses a stream of dark brown frothy water called Adam's Ale.

At the 2km (1.2-mile) point you reach a junction that marks the end of a loop you can take on the return trip. For now, keep right on the main trail.

Soon afterward, you will get your first view of Western Brook Pond itself, although the massive cliffs rising up from the sides of the lake have been visible since the beginning. The dock is reached after 3km (2 miles); there are restrooms, a shelter and picnic tables here. The boat tour goes right to the far end of the lake, where backpackers can be dropped off.

On the return trip, you can follow the alternative trail beside the lake (this adds about another 1km/0.6 mile to the total distance).

After 1km (0.6 mile), you reach the edge of Western Brook itself as it leaves the lake. In the summer months, a suspension bridge crosses the stream.

Don't cross the bridge, but instead continue to follow the stream. After a further 2km (1.2 miles), you rejoin the main trail, and 4km (2.5 miles) after leaving the dock you return to the parking area.

Distance
7km (4.3 miles) round trip (including optional loop)

Time
Walk: 2 hours. Boat trip: 2.5 hours

Start/end point
Parking area on Route 430, 32km (20 miles) north of Park Visitor Centre in Rocky Harbour
✚ 29B3

Lunch
Buy a picnic in Rocky Harbour

Boat tour
☎ 709/458-2730 (reservations recommended)
🕐 Daily 10 am, 1 pm, 4 pm, Jul–Aug; 1 pm, late Jun and early Sep
♿ Few
✋ Expensive

Wildlife Trail
The well-maintained trail leading to Western Brook Pond crosses coastal lowland that is alive with low-growing plants such as wild orchids, blue flag irises, bakeapple and cranberry in season. It rises gently several times over limestone ridges covered with stunted spruce and fir, and descends into boggy areas (there are boardwalks across these). Although you will see the droppings of bear, moose and caribou, you will be lucky to see them in the flesh.

Cliffs loom over Western Brook Pond

37

The Officers Quarters, King's Bastion, Louisbourg

www.gov.nf.ca/tourism
🗺 29A4
ℹ️ Newfoundland and Labrador Department of Tourism, P.O. Box 8700, St. John's, Newfoundland and Labrador, A1B 4J6
☎ 800/563-6353 toll free

Red Bay National Historic Site

www.parkscanada.gc.ca
✉ P.O. Box 103, Red Bay, Newfoundland and Labrador, A0K 4K0
☎ 709/920-2142
🕐 Daily, mid-Jun to mid-Oct
♿ Good 💵 Moderate

www.parkscanada.gc.ca
🗺 29B2
✉ 259 Park Service Road, Louisbourg, Nova Scotia, B1C 2L2
☎ 902/733-2280
🕐 Daily. Animation: daily, late May–early Oct
🍴 Restaurants ($–$$)
♿ Good
💵 Expensive late May–early Oct; free rest of year (buildings closed)
❓ Craft demonstrations, military drills, etc.

HOPEWELL ROCKS (▶ 18, TOP TEN)

LABRADOR

A land of towering mountains, huge lakes and fast-flowing rivers, Labrador is one of the world's few remaining true wilderness areas. It stretches from the Strait of Belle Isle to the shores of Ungava Bay, a distance of nearly 1,000km (more than 600 miles), and it covers a staggering 1,560,000sq km (more than 600,000 square miles). Much of the region is inaccessible. A ferry from St. Barbe on the island of Newfoundland to Blanc Sablon in Québec enables you to access the Labrador coast and drive up it for a short distance.

Red Bay (78km/48 miles from the ferry) was the whaling capital of the world in the 16th century. Dozens of Basque fishermen came here to hunt right and bowhead whales in order to supply Europe with oil for lamps and soap. An interpretation center re-creates these times.

LOUISBOURG ⭐⭐⭐

At one time, Louisbourg was the great fortress of New France, guarding the entrance to the St. Lawrence River and the colony. Constructed in the early 18th century, it had the largest garrison in North America. Captured and destroyed by the British in 1758, the fort lay in ruins for two centuries, but today it has risen from the ashes. Covering 4.8 hectares (12 acres), the site now holds a faithful re-creation of a town of the 1740s, with impressive walls and gates. From the visitor center you have to walk or take a shuttle bus to the entrance. The 50-plus buildings are of wood or roughcast masonry, furnished in 1740s style and populated with suitably attired "residents." Tour the King's Bastion and visit the governor's elegant apartments, and be sure not to miss the soldiers' barracks – even though they aren't conducive to a long stay!

A Drive Along the Cabot Trail

This spectacular circular tour hugs the coast – sometimes high above it, sometimes at sea level – with stunning views of ocean, mountains and forest, and opportunities for viewing moose, bald eagles, whales and a multitude of seabirds. Distances are given from the start of the drive, except where stated.

From Baddeck, drive east, turning right onto the Cabot Trail at Nyanza (8km/5 miles). Follow the Margaree River to the coast (60km/37 miles) and continue to Chéticamp.

Chéticamp is the center of the region's Acadian culture and gateway to Cape Breton Highlands National Park (8km/5 miles from town), where one of the most spectacular parts of the drive begins.

Climb 450m (1,475 feet) over French and Mackenzie mountains, then descend along switchbacks to Pleasant Bay (123km/76 miles). Heading inland, climb steeply over North Mountain and then descend to the coast along the valley of the North Aspy River (171km/106 miles). Take the 2km (1.2-mile) detour to Neil's Harbour to picnic by the lighthouse. After lunch, return to the main trail and drive to Black Brook Cove.

Walk to the beach here to see pink granite rocks stretching into the sea. In Ingonish (21km/13 miles beyond Black Brook Cove), visit the grounds of Keltic Lodge resort hotel and walk out onto Middle Head, famous for its seabird colonies.

Climb steeply up Cape Smokey and from its top admire the view of Ingonish and its bay. Descend vertiginously to sea level again, continuing south along the Gaelic Coast.

In South Gut St. Ann's (272km/169 miles) is Gaelic College, the only school in North America to teach Gaelic and the arts and crafts of the Scottish Highlands.

Return to Baddeck (292km/181 miles).

Distance
292km (181 miles), excluding detour

Time
1 day (at least)

Start/end point
Baddeck on Trans-Canada Highway 1
✚ 29B2

Lunch
Buy a picnic in Chéticamp

Cape Breton Highlands National Park
www.parkscanada.gc.ca/cape bretonhighlands
✉ Ingonish Beach, Nova Scotia, B0C 1L0
☎ 902/224-2306 (seasonal), 902/285-2691 (year-round)
◷ Daily
🍴 Restaurant Acadien in Chéticamp (► 81); Ingonish ($–$$$)
♿ Good
💲 Moderate mid-May to mid-Oct; free mid-Oct to mid-May

The Cabot Trail south of Neil's Harbour

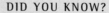

www.explorelunenburg.ca
🕂 29B1
✉ Blockhouse Road
☎ 902/634-8100

Fisheries Museum of the Atlantic
www.novascotiamuseums
✉ 68 Bluenose Drive
☎ 902/634-4794
🕐 Daily, May–Oct; Mon–Fri, rest of year
🍽 Old Fish Factory ($$)
♿ Good 💰 Expensive

www.peiplay.com
🕂 29B2
✉ Box 940, Charlottetown, Prince Edward Island, C1A 7M5 ☎ 902/368-7795

Green Gables House
www.pc.gc.ca
✉ Cavendish, Prince Edward Island National Park
☎ 902/963-7874
🕐 Daily, May–Oct
🍽 Restaurants nearby ($–$$)
♿ Few 💰 Moderate

LUNENBURG

Set on a steep hillside and characterized by narrow streets and colorful wood-framed buildings, Lunenburg radiates the flavor of its seafaring heritage. One of Nova Scotia's most attractive towns and a UNESCO World Heritage Site since 1995, it has a waterfront active with the fishing and shipbuilding industries that have been the backbone of its prosperity since its foundation in 1753. The bright red buildings of the **Fisheries Museum of the Atlantic** commemorate this heritage, and offer interesting displays and activities. In the summer months, the schooner *Bluenose II* is often in the port. Visitors can board her for a boat trip.

PRINCE EDWARD ISLAND

Tiny Prince Edward Island (known as PEI) has quiet rural landscapes, bright red soil and fine sandy beaches. Connected to the mainland since 1997 by Confederation Bridge (above), PEI's fame has spread worldwide as the setting for the children's classic, *Anne of Green Gables*. Lucy Maud Montgomery wrote 19 novels featuring PEI, but none is as famous as the one starring the young orphan redhead. People come from the ends of the Earth to see "Anne's Island," and no trip is complete without visiting **Green Gables**, the small white and green house that is furnished to reflect the story. It is located in Prince Edward Island National Park, which also has splendid sand dunes and beaches.

The island's gracious capital, Charlottetown, is a delightful place to saunter around, with its fine homes and tree-lined streets. The rest of the island can be explored by following some of the well-signed scenic drives, and don't miss taking part in a lobster supper (available across the island).

Green Gables House, Cavendish – one of the most visited homes in Canada

ST. ANDREWS-BY-THE-SEA ⭐⭐

Pleasantly situated at the end of a peninsula extending into Passamaquoddy Bay, St. Andrews-by-the-Sea is a charming community. Settled by Loyalists in 1783, its tree-lined streets are named after King George III's 15 children. Later, St. Andrews became a fashionable place for wealthy Canadians to build summer homes. It is also the location of New Brunswick's major resort, the Algonquin Hotel.

Take a stroll along Water Street, the quaint main thoroughfare, with its collection of interesting little stores and restaurants. Wander up and down the older streets for close-ups of their well-proportioned Georgian houses (some are open to the public). St. Andrews is also affected by the high tides of the Bay of Fundy (▶ 18, Top Ten, and 36), which can best be viewed from the town wharf.

ST. JOHN'S ⭐⭐⭐

Facing the open Atlantic in the extreme east of Newfoundland, the province's capital has a spectacular site on the slopes of a natural harbor. The steep, narrow streets are a clutter of brightly colored wooden houses and the harbor is full of the ships of many nations. St. John's is rocky, treeless and windblown, but it has a very special character. Its inhabitants, many of whom are of Irish descent, have a distinctive accent and a great sense of humor; and they adore their city.

From the harbor, there are boat trips to view whales and the giant icebergs that float past in early summer. Peek inside the Murray Premises, renovated fishing warehouses built in 1846 (▶ 99), and on the road to Signal Hill (▶ 24, Top Ten) note the entrance to the **Johnson Geo Centre**, a sensational geological showcase constructed underground. Displays here explain why the province of Newfoundland and Labrador is so spectacular in geological terms.

---

www.
townsearch.com/standrews
🔝 29A1
ℹ️ St. Andrews Chamber of Commerce: 46 Reed Avenue, St. Andrews-by-the-Sea, New Brunswick, E5B 1A1 ☎ 506/529-3555
↔️ Fundy National Park (▶ 36)

Above: St. Andrews is lined with picturesque cottages and homes

---

🔝 29C3
ℹ️ City Hall 2nd Floor Annex, 35 New Gower Street, St. John's, Newfoundland and Labrador, A1C 5M2 ☎ 709/576-8106

Johnson Geo Centre
www.geocentre.ca
✉️ 175 Signal Hill Road
☎ 709/737-7880
🕐 Daily, Jun to mid-Oct; Tue–Sun, rest of year
♿ Very good
🍴 Moderate
↔️ Avalon Peninsula (▶ 34)
❓ Geo-boutique with geologal items

Traditional crafts are practised at Village Historique Acadien

www.
parkscanada.gc.ca/terranova
✚ 29C3
✉ Glovertown,
Newfoundland and
Labrador, A0G 2L0.
240km (149 miles) from
St. John's
☎ 709/533-2801
🕐 Daily
🚢 For boat tours on
Newman Sound, contact
Ocean Watch Tours:
709/533-6024
♿ Few
💲 Moderate mid-May to
mid-Oct; free rest of year

www.
villagehistoriqueacadien.com
✚ 29A2
✉ P.O. Box 5626, Caraquet,
New Brunswick, E1W
1B7. 10km (6 miles) west
of Caraquet in
northeastern New
Brunswick
☎ 506/726-2600, 877/721-
2200 (toll-free)
🕐 Daily, Jun to mid-Oct
(reduction of services
from early Sep)
🍽 Restaurant and food
services ($–$$)
♿ Good
💲 Expensive
❓ Store selling Acadian
items

TERRA NOVA NATIONAL PARK

At Terra Nova, on the east coast of Newfoundland, forested hills meet sheltered fingers of the sea that penetrate deep inland, creating an area rich in wildlife and scenic beauty. Moose, lynx and black bear haunt the forests, bald eagles and great horned owls soar overhead, and whales and other marine life frequent the waters offshore.

Terra Nova is easily accessible, since the Trans-Canada Highway bisects it. Most park facilities are located on Newman Sound, including the Marine Interpretation Centre in Saltons, where you can journey from a shoreline habitat to the depths of the ocean. There are also boat tours, which provide opportunities for observing different aspects of the life of the Sound, and several excellent viewpoints on land.

VILLAGE HISTORIQUE ACADIEN

Located on New Brunswick's Acadian Peninsula near Caraquet, this re-created village provides an authentic representation of French Acadian life between 1770 and 1939. The story of the Acadians is a sad one. Expelled from their rich farmlands in Nova Scotia in 1755, most of these French settlers were forcibly deported into the British colonies farther south. Some then eventually made their way north again to settle in this area of New Brunswick.

Acadian pride in their heritage comes through strongly at Village Historique Acadien. Here, more than 40 buildings are staffed by interpreters in period costume, who bring the place to life by talking about their customs and trades. You can watch a tinsmith or woodworker at work, or listen to a printer explaining his business. Traditional Acadian food can be sampled at La Table des Ancêtres restaurant, the gift store is full of Acadian crafts, and you can even stay overnight on site at the Château Albert.

Québec

The heart of French Canada, the province of Québec is simply gigantic, extending 1,900km (1,200 miles) north from the U.S. border to the shores of the Hudson Strait. A land of sharp contrasts, it is resolutely distinct in its culture and lifestyle. Traversed by the magnificent St. Lawrence, one of the world's great rivers, it boasts some spectacular scenery. The Gaspé Peninsula has awe-inspiring seascapes, Saguenay Fjord is bounded by impressive cliffs and filled with dark waters, and the Charlevoix coast offers sweeping views of river and hinterland. Elsewhere, visitors can enjoy the tranquility of the Eastern Townships or the bustling sports-oriented ambience of the Laurentians. Add to these cosmopolitan, sophisticated Montréal, with its great restaurants and never-ending summer festivals, and the old-world charm of the capital, Québec City, and the great diversity of the province can be fully appreciated.

'You who, in stanzas, celebrate the Po,
Or teach the Tiber in your strains to flow,
How would you toil for numbers to proclaim
The liquid grandeur of St. Lawrence' Stream?'

J. Mackay
From *"Quebec Hill; Or Canadian Scenery. A Poem. In Two Parts"*
(1797)

─────────── ● ───────────

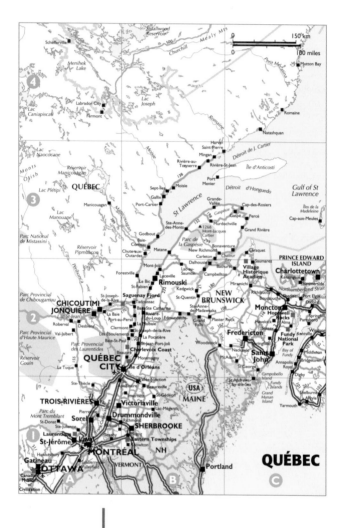

Montréal ✪✪✪

A mighty metropolis set on an island in the St. Lawrence, Montréal is urbane, sophisticated and cosmopolitan, and its inhabitants believe passionately in the *joie de vivre*. Although this is the second-largest French-speaking city in the world, fully one-third of the population is non-French, giving it a tremendous cultural vitality.

In 1642, Ville-Marie de Montréal was founded as a Roman Catholic mission; even a hundred years ago it was dominated by the towers and spires of its churches, gaining it the moniker "the city of one hundred steeples." This religious heritage is still evident in the city's churches, even though they stand empty today. It is also evident in the huge cross on top of Mont-Royal, illuminated at night.

In 1760, the British conquered the city and the economy became the domain of a group of industrious Scots. They expanded the fur trade, founded banks, built the railroads and left their mark on the city architecturally in the form of splendid stone and brick buildings. The late 20th century saw the "reconquest" of the city by the Québécois, and its face has now changed to one that is resolutely French.

Today, Montréal's economy is vibrant, with a strong high-tech orientation and a major port despite its location a thousand miles from the open ocean. The downtown area is flourishing, with the construction of some magnificent buildings, all interconnected by the passageways and plazas of the Underground City, born of Montréal's long, cold winter, which has an average snowfall of 3m (nearly 10 feet), more than any other major city on Earth.

www.tourisme-montreal.org
🗺 44A1

Centre Infotouriste
🏠 1001 du Square Dorchester, Montréal, Québec, H3B 1N1
☎ 514/873-2015, 877/266-5687 (toll free)
🕐 Daily
Ⓜ Peel

Montréal's striking mixture of modern and historic buildings

The magnificent interior of Basilique Notre-Dame

🞧 44A1
✉ 110 rue Notre-Dame Ouest
☎ 514/842-2950, 866/842-2925 (toll-free)
🕐 Daily. Sound and light shows: Tue–Sat evenings
♿ Good
🍴 Restaurants nearby ($–$$$)
Ⓜ Place d'Armes
💰 Moderate (no charge for attending Mass)
Vieux-Montréal (➤ 51)
❓ Guided tours. Religious gift store

---

www.
marguerite-bourgeoys.com
🞧 44A1
✉ 400 rue St-Paul Est
☎ 514/282-8670
🕐 Daily; closed mid-Jan to Feb
🍴 Restaurants nearby ($–$$$)
Ⓜ Champ-de-Mars
♿ Good
💰 Free. Museum: moderate
Summer theatrical presentations; winter concerts

What to See in Montréal

BASILIQUE NOTRE-DAME DE MONTRÉAL
(NOTRE-DAME BASILICA)

The twin towers of Montréal's most famous Catholic church rise over 69m (226 feet) on the south side of place d'Armes. Once they dominated the whole city, but in recent years they have been dwarfed by the surrounding financial institutions. Built in 1823–29, this neo-Gothic edifice was designed by James O'Donnell, an Irishman from New York who, surprisingly, was a Protestant.

The extraordinary interior of the church was the masterpiece of Victor Bourgeau, a local architect. It is handcarved in wood, mainly red pine, and decorated with 22-carat gold. Above the main altar, the reredos features scenes of sacrifice from the Bible sculpted in white pine. On the left side is the massive pulpit, decorated with sculptures of saints and prophets. Behind the main altar, don't miss the Chapelle du Sacre Coeur (Sacred Heart Chapel), rebuilt in 1982 after a fire. It is dominated by an enormous 15m-high (50-foot) bronze depicting humanity's journey through life towards heaven, the work of Charles Daudelin.

CHAPELLE NOTRE-DAME-DE-BONSECOURS
(CHAPEL OF NOTRE-DAME-DE-BONSECOURS) ⭐⭐

Located on the waterfront, this little church has been a Montréal landmark for many years. In the 19th century, sailors adopted it as their special church and a large statue of the Virgin with arms outstretched faces the river. Inside, don't miss the magnificent grisaille frescoes, painted directly onto the wooden vault by François-Édouard Meloche in 1886. They recount scenes in the life of the Virgin and are executed in a *trompe l'oeil* style. The adjoining museum is devoted to Marguerite Bourgeoys, who settled in Montréal in 1653, built the original chapel on this site, and was canonized in 1982. There is a magnificent view of the river and harbor from the church tower.

CHRIST CHURCH
(CATHÉDRALE ÉPISCOPALE DE CHRIST CHURCH) ✪

Squeezed in between towering office blocks and under-pinned by a large shopping center, this Anglican cathedral (built between 1856 and 1859) is a fine example of neo-Gothic architecture. It has a flamboyant triple portico on rue Ste-Catherine decorated with gables, gargoyles and grotesques, and an attractive courtyard cloister at the back. Inside, walk up the nave below Gothic arches into the chancel, which has a copy of Leonardo da Vinci's *Last Supper*. Just above the pulpit, note the cross created from nails collected in the ruins of England's Coventry Cathedral after it was bombed in 1940.

JARDIN BOTANIQUE DE MONTRÉAL
(MONTRÉAL BOTANICAL GARDENS) ✪✪✪

Considered the finest of their type in North America, these splendid gardens extend over 73 hectares (180 acres). They consist of nearly 30 thematic gardens featuring more than 22,000 different species, creating a veritable living museum of plants from the four corners of the Earth. The extraordinary Chinese Garden includes a number of pagodas set around a lake, while the serene Japanese Garden also has a lake, plus a rock fountain and tea house. The First Nations Garden has winding paths, masses of trees and a lake populated with wildfowl. In summer, the gardens of annuals and perennials, and the rose garden, are glorious. There are also 10 conservatories featuring magnificent orchids, tropical plants, ferns and bonsai. The large Arboretum has a tree house with interesting displays, while the Insectarium is a unique museum devoted to the insect world, with both live and dead specimens.

MONT-ROYAL ✪✪✪

Set on the north slope of Mont-Royal is the shrine of **L'Oratoire St-Joseph** (St. Joseph's Oratory), whose huge dome is visible from all over the city. Founded in 1904, it is visited by millions of pilgrims every year. (For Mont-Royal Chalet, ➤ 19, Top Ten.)

www.
montreal.anglican.org/cathedral
🔲 44A1
✉ 635 rue Ste-Catherine Ouest
☎ 514/843-6577
🕐 Daily
🍴 Restaurant in shopping mall beneath cathedral ($)
Ⓜ McGill
♿ Good
🎟 Free
↔ Underground City (➤ 50)
❓ Lunchtime concerts

🔲 44A1
www.
ville.montreal.qc.ca/jardin
✉ 4101 rue Sherbrooke Est
☎ 514/872-1400
🕐 Daily, 9–sunset
🍴 Cafeteria ($)
Ⓔ Pie IX, Viau then free shuttle bus
♿ Excellent
🎟 Expensive May–Oct; free outdoors rest of year. Parking charge
↔ Parc olympique (➤ 49)
❓ Guided tours; *balade* (small train) tour (free). Horticultural gift store

The Dream Lake Garden in the Jardin Botanique, gift of the city of Shanghai

🔲 44A1

L'Oratoire St-Joseph de Mont-Royal
www.saint-joseph.org
✉ 3800 Chemin Queen-Mary
☎ 514/733-8211
🕐 Daily
🍴 Cafeteria ($)
Ⓔ Côte-des-Neiges
♿ Good
❓ Religious gift store

➕ 44A1
www.pacmuseum.qc.ca
✉ 350 place Royale
☎ 514/872-9150
🕐 Daily, late Jun–early Sep; Tue–Sun, rest of year
🍴 Restaurant l'Arrivage ($$)
Ⓜ Place d'Armes
♿ Good
👋 Expensive
↔ Vieux-Montréal (▶ 51)
🛍 Boutique with gifts and books

MUSÉE D'ARCHÉOLOGIE ET D'HISTOIRE DE MONTRÉAL (POINTE-À-CALLIÈRE MUSEUM OF ARCHEOLOGY AND HISTORY) ★★

Set on the point of land in Old Montréal where the city started life in 1642, this is an intriguing museum in a striking modern building. A multimedia presentation (15 minutes) provides an introduction to the history of the site. Then you can proceed underground into an archeological crypt to inspect remains of the old city walls and buildings that have stood on this site since the 17th century. You'll meet some former residents in the form of laser holograms, who will answer your questions in French or English. Climb the stairs into the old Customs House for more exhibitions, or take the elevator up the tower to a great viewpoint overlooking the river and harbor.

➕ 44A1
www.macm.org
✉ 185 rue Ste-Catherine Ouest
☎ 514/847-6226
🕐 Tue–Sun
🍴 Restaurants nearby ($–$$)
Ⓜ Place-des-Arts
♿ Very good
👋 Moderate
↔ Underground City (▶ 50)
🛍 Art bookstore and art-oriented gift store

MUSÉE D'ART CONTEMPORAIN (MUSEUM OF CONTEMPORARY ART) ★

Montréal's contemporary art museum is part of the downtown performing arts complex at place-des-Arts, which also includes theaters and a concert hall. The museum building is recognizable by the pair of giant lips on its roof, called *La Voie lactée (The Milky Way)*, an artwork by Geneviève Cadieux. This is the only museum in Canada devoted solely to contemporary art, and its approach is innovative. It hosts exhibitions featuring new media such as video, film, contemporary dance and theater, as well as more traditional artistic means of expression.

The Musée d'art contemporain specializes in innovative exhibits

MUSÉE DES BEAUX-ARTS DE MONTRÉAL (MONTRÉAL MUSEUM OF FINE ARTS) ✪✪✪

With its encyclopedic collection of art dating from antiquity to contemporary times, the Montréal Museum of Fine Arts is located downtown in buildings on Sherbrooke Street. On the north side of the street, a Beaux-Arts building of 1912 houses the Canadian Collection, including some splendid Inuit works, and the Decorative Arts Galleries. Across the street is Moshe Safdie's 1991 pavilion, which houses the galleries of European and contemporary art, as well as temporary exhibitions. Connecting the two are vast underground vaults lined with works of ancient civilizations (China, Japan and the Middle East), and African and pre-Columbian art. The museum is particularly renowned for its blockbuster temporary shows.

www.mmfa.qc.ca
🚏 44A1
✉ 1379–1380 rue Sherbrooke Ouest
☎ 514/285-2000, 800/899-6873 (toll-free)
🕐 Tue–Sun, holiday Mons 11–5
🍽 Restaurant ($$$), cafeteria ($)
🚇 Guy-Concordia
🚌 Bus 24
♿ Excellent
🎫 Permanent collection: free. Temporary exhibits: expensive

PARC JEAN-DRAPEAU (JEAN-DRAPEAU PARK) ✪✪

This park is composed of two islands and has a superb location in the middle of the St. Lawrence River that offers unparalleled views of the city. Together, Île Ste-Hélène and Île Notre-Dame provided the site for the 1967 World's Fair (Expo 67). Two of the former pavilions remain: the France pavilion houses the Montréal Casino; and the U.S.A. pavilion, Buckminster Fuller's geodesic dome, which contains the Biosphère, an environmental museum (► 111). The La Ronde amusement park, with thrilling rides, is also located here.

www.parcjeandrapeau.com
🚏 44A1
✉ 1 circuit Gilles-Villeneuve
☎ 514/872-6120
🕐 Daily. La Ronde: daily, late May–early Sep
🚇 Jean-Drapeau
🚌 Bus 169 for access to islands, 167 on islands
⛴ Ferry from Vieux-Port Jun–early Sep
🎫 La Ronde: expensive

PARC OLYMPIQUE (OLYMPIC PARK) ✪✪

Site of the summer Olympic games of 1976, Olympic Park is dominated by a huge elliptical stadium that sports a leaning tower and strange roof. Controversial because of its cost, it is nonetheless a remarkable building and the view of the city from the top of the tower is nothing short of spectacular. Beside the stadium stands the Biodôme, which was used for the cycling events of the Olympic games. Today, it houses a fascinating indoor zoological park with animals, birds and fish from a series of different ecosystems (► 110).

www.rio.gouv.qc.ca
🚏 44A1
✉ 4141 avenue Pierre-de-Coubertin
☎ 514/252-4141
🕐 Daily
🍽 Café
🚇 Pie IX, Viau
♿ Good
🎫 Guided tours, ascent of tower and Biodôme admission: all expensive
↔ Jardin botanique de Montréal (► 47)
❓ Ball games and other sports events; trade shows

The Biosphère, with the city in the background

44A1
Centre Infotouriste: 1001
du Square Dorchester,
Montréal, Québec, H3B
1N1 ☎ 514/873-2015,
877/266-5687 (toll-free)
Peel

*Leafy Square Dorchester
– in the heart of Montréal*

SQUARE DORCHESTER (DORCHESTER SQUARE) ★

Attractive buildings surround this square, which sits in the heart of downtown Montréal. On the northern side stands the Florentine-inspired Dominion Square Building, housing the tourist information office; to the east is the silver-granite "wedding cake" Sun Life Building; and to the west is the Second Empire former Windsor Hotel and the 45-story CIBC tower, built in 1962. The south side is dominated by the Roman Catholic Cathedral of Marie-Reine-du-Monde, a reproduction in miniature of St. Peter's in Rome and built between 1870 and 1894. Inside the cathedral, note the replica of Gian Lorenzo Bernini's baroque baldachin over the altar and the dramatic paintings by Georges Delfosse, representing episodes in the history of the Canadian Catholic Church.

44A1
For details and maps,
contact Centre
Infotouriste: 1001 du
Square Dorchester,
Montréal, Québec, H3B
1N1 ☎ 514/873-2015,
877/266-5687 (toll-free)

UNDERGROUND CITY (VILLE SOUTERRAINE) ★★

Montréalers have learned to cope with their harsh winters – up to 3m (10 feet) of snow fall and temperatures dip to -35°C (-31°F) – by developing a weatherproof system in the downtown area that gives priority to pedestrians. This network of passageways, atriums and wide open spaces, which extends for more than 30km (20 miles) and connects more than 60 buildings and eight métro stations, is known as the Underground City, although not all of it is strictly underground.

It all started with place Ville-Marie, the huge cruciform tower designed by I. M. Pei in 1962. Highlights here include Le Complexe Les Ailes, with an enormous skylight that cuts right through the building; Promenades Cathèdrale, an architecturally impressive complex below Christ Church cathedral (► 47); the elegant Cours Mont-Royal complex, with its enclosed courtyards; the tallest building in the city, 1000 de la Gauchetière, with a spectacular indoor skating rink; and the high, light and luminous Centre de Commerce mondial de Montréal.

VIEUX-MONTRÉAL (OLD MONTRÉAL) ✪✪✪

Located close to the river, Old Montréal is a district of narrow, cobblestoned streets and old houses. It is the original French city, and today has been transformed into a picturesque and attractive area that you can visit either by horse-drawn carriage or on foot.

Don't miss place Jacques Cartier, with its outdoor cafés, street performers, musicians and flower vendors, a particularly lively spot on summer evenings. At the north end of the square stands Montréal's magnificent Hôtel-de-Ville (City Hall), built in the French Second Empire style. Across the street is the venerable Château Ramezay, built in 1705 as a residence for the governor of Montréal and today housing a museum devoted to local history – the basement has huge stone vaults. Nearby, on rue St-Paul, is the Marché Bonsecours, with a Renaissance-style dome. Its name comes from the chapel next door, Notre-Dame-de-Bonsecours (➤ 46). The building has been converted into a marketplace for local designers and craftspeople, and also houses several restaurants. Finally, don't miss place d'Armes, where the Notre-Dame Basilica (➤ 46) takes pride of place.

VIEUX-PORT (OLD PORT) ✪✪

The Old Port is the name given to the area beside the St. Lawrence River south of rue de la Commune, which today forms an attractive linear waterfront park offering great views of the city and river. A range of activities is available, from cycling and walking paths to boat trips and iceskating in winter. Exhibitions and festivals of all types are held here throughout the year, and there is also the Centre des sciences de Montréal (Montréal Science Centre; ➤ 111) with its IMAX movie theater to visit. The 45m-high (145-foot) **Tour de l'Horloge** (Clock Tower), beside the river, can be climbed (192 steps) for a splendid view of the city.

Sidebar

➕ 44A1
ℹ️ Centre Infotouriste (Vieux-Montréal): 174 rue Notre-Dame Est (on corner of place Jacques Cartier) ☎ 514/873-2015
🍴 Restaurants ($–$$$)
🚇 Champ-de-Mars, place d'Armes, Square Victoria
♿ Few
↔️ Vieux-Port (➤ below)

Below: *The Vieux-Port is one of the city's most visited attractions*

www.oldportofmontreal.com
➕ 44A1
✉️ 333 rue de la Commune Ouest, Montréal, Québec, H2Y 2E2
☎ 514/496-7678, 800/971-7678 (toll-free)
🍴 Cafés ($)
🚇 Champ-de-Mars, place d'Armes, Square Victoria
♿ Good
↔️ Vieux-Montréal (➤ above)

Tour de l'Horloge
www.oldportofmontreal.com
✉️ quai de l'Horloge, Vieux-Port de Montréal
☎ 514/496-7678, 800/971-7678 (toll-free)
🕐 Daily, late May–early Oct
♿ None
🎫 Free
↔️ Vieux-Montréal (➤ above)

Québec City ✪✪✪

Citadel, seaport and provincial capital, Canada's oldest city is built on a rock above the St. Lawrence. It has a distinct European flavor, with impressive fortifications and narrow cobblestoned streets lined with grey-stone buildings. True to its claim as the birthplace of French culture in North America, Québec City offers excellent restaurants, lively cafés and a vibrant nightlife.

www.regiondequebec.com
➕ 44B2

Centre Infotouriste
ℹ️ 12 rue Ste-Anne, Québec City, Québec, G1R 3X2

In 1608, Samuel de Champlain built a trading settlement at the point "where the river narrows" (the meaning of the word Québec). Over the next 150 years, his settlement grew in size and importance to become the center of all activities in New France, an empire that stretched through the Great Lakes and south to the Gulf of Mexico. In 1759, a British fleet arrived under the command of James Wolfe and scaled the great rock face that provided Québec with its natural defense. The ensuing battle on the Plains of Abraham was won by the British, deciding the fate not only of the city but of the whole continent.

Today, it is a joy to explore Québec City's Haute-Ville, at the top of the cliff, and the Basse-Ville, below it at the foot. The steep cliffs are still impressive despite the construction of port facilities at their base, and the former battlefield of the Plains of Abraham offers a magnificent park covering 100 hectares (250 acres), with woodland, formal gardens and sweeping views of the St. Lawrence. In 1985, the combination of fortified site and French culture gave Québec a place on UNESCO's World Heritage List, one of only two Canadian cities to receive this honor.

Tourist Information
ℹ️ 835 avenue Wilfred-Laurier, Québec G1R 2L3
☎️ 418/649-2608

Above: *the brass band of the Canada 22e regiment performing in front of the Citadel*

Opposite: *Promenade des Gouverneurs*

53

The sumptuous interior of Cathédrale Notre-Dame

www.
patrimoine-religieux.com

✠ 44B2

✉ 29 rue de Buade

☎ 418/694-0665

🕐 Daily 7:30–4:30. Sound and light shows: daily, May to mid-Oct

♿ Good

🎫 Free. Sound and light shows: expensive

↔ Château Frontenac (► below)

❓ Guided tours May–Oct

www.fairmont.com

✠ 44B2

✉ 1 rue des Carrières

☎ 418/692-3861, 800/441-1414 (toll-free)

♿ Very good

↔ Terrasse Dufferin (► 25, Top Ten)

❓ Guided tours (expensive and popular; reservations ☎ 418/691-2166)

CATHÉDRALE NOTRE-DAME DE QUÉBEC (NOTRE-DAME CATHEDRAL) ⊘

The Roman Catholic Cathedral of Notre-Dame has a rather undistinguished neoclassical façade that belies the opulence of the interior with its gold decoration. Over the altar, a vast wooden canopy is finished in gold, as are the pulpit and the bishop's throne. On the right side, a funeral chapel honors Monsignor de Laval, the first bishop of Québec; a map of his diocese – which extended over half the continent – is etched on the floor.

This is the third cathedral on this site. The first was destroyed by British bombardments in 1759, while the second was burned down in 1922. Rising like a phoenix from the ashes, the present cathedral stands on the same foundations and was rebuilt using the original plans.

CHÂTEAU FRONTENAC ⊘⊘

Inextricably linked with the image of the city, the Château Frontenac is one of Canada's most famous and easily recognizable hotels. Named after a French governor, the Comte de Frontenac, it towers flamboyantly above its surroundings, a magnificent structure of turrets, towers and copper roofs. The original hotel was built by Bruce Price for the Canadian Pacific Railway in 1893, and its architecture gave rise to the term "château style," subsequently used for hotels right across the country.

Even if you are not staying here, step inside to see the interior (► 101). During World War II, the hotel hosted the Québec Conferences, when the Normandy landings were planned by U.S. President Franklin D. Roosevelt and British Prime Minister Winston Churchill.

CHUTE MONTMORENCY (MONTMORENCY FALLS) ✪✪✪

Near its junction with the St. Lawrence, the Montmorency River cascades over a cliff in an impressive waterfall. These falls are 83m (272 feet) high, and the spray they create forms a great cone of ice in the winter known as the *pain de sucre* (sugarloaf); this can be up to 30m (100 feet) high. Tobogganing down the cone became a tradition in the 19th century and continues to this day.

Parc de la Chute Montmorency offers viewpoints at both the top and the bottom of the falls. At the top, a boardwalk takes you to a suspension bridge across the cataract that has spectacular views. At the bottom, you can walk right up to the whirlpool at the base of the falls – so long as you don't mind being drenched by the spray. A cable car connects the upper and lower levels, or you can pass between the two via a steep staircase (487 steps). The Manoir Montmorency at the top houses an interpretive center and restaurant.

CITADELLE (QUÉBEC CITADEL) ✪✪

This vast four-pointed polygon extends over 15 hectares (37 acres) and remains an active military base, home to the Royal 22e Régiment. It took the British more than 30 years (1820–50) to complete the construction of the vast array of earthworks and bastions that make up the fort, following a design by the French military architect Vauban. The Citadel encloses two buildings that date from the French regime, plus numerous others that were added later.

To visit the Citadel, you must join a guided tour (it is impossible to visit it independently). Buildings bearing the names of the various campaigns of the Royal 22e Régiment (Vimy, the Somme, Normandy, Korea and so on) surround a huge parade ground where military ceremonies take place. Located in a powder magazine dating from 1750 is a museum presenting military insignia, weapons, uniforms and an excellent diorama showing the various battles fought at Québec.

From the Citadel, an entire network of walls and gates encircles the old part of the city, stretching a total of 4.6km (2.8 miles) – see the walk on page 60.

Military hardware on display at the Citadelle

www.
chutemontmorency.qc.ca
✛ 44B2
⊠ Parc de la Chute Montmorency, 2490 avenue Royal, Beauport
☎ 418/663-3330
🕐 Upper Park: daily. Cable car and Lower Park: daily, Apr–Oct
🍴 Restaurant ($$)
🚌 Bus 50, 53
♿ Good
🅿 Parkin____ expens____ expens____
↔ Ste-An____ (► 57___
❓ Craft s____ (6 mile___

www.laci____
✛ 44B2
⊠ Côte___ 6020___ Ville___
☎ 418/___
🕐 Guid___ Apr–___ Guard ceremonics: daily 10 am sharp, late Jun–early Sep
♿ Good
🅿 Moderate

www.ogs.net/cathedral
✚ 44B2
✉ 31 rue des Jardins
☎ 418/692-2193
🕐 Daily, May to mid-Oct;
open for services, by
arrangement, or by
chance, rest of year.
Guided tours: Jul–Aug.
Craft stalls: Jul–Aug
🍴 Nearby ($–$$)
♿ Good
🎟 Free
↔ Cathédrale Notre-Dame
de Québec (▶ 54)

www.mcq.org (in French)
✚ 44B2
✉ 85 rue Dalhousie, C.P.
155, Succursale B
☎ 418/643-2158
🕐 Daily, late Jun–early Sep;
Tue–Sun, rest of year
🍴 Cafeteria ($)
♿ Excellent
🎟 Expensive; free Tue, mid-
Sep to mid-Jun
↔ Place Royale
(▶ opposite)
❓ Gift store in Maison
Estèbe

Historic place Royale,
lined by stately old
houses

HOLY TRINITY ANGLICAN CATHEDRAL
(CATHÉDRALE ÉPISCOPALE DE LA STE-TRINITÉ) ✪

Consecrated in 1804, this wood-framed Georgian church was the first Anglican cathedral to be built outside the British Isles. Modeled on the church of St. Martin-in-the-Fields in central London, it was paid for by King George III and still boasts a royal pew reserved for the sovereign. The light and spacious interior has box pews made of oak transported from England's royal forests. There is an impressive collection of stained glass: In the chancel, the triptych window portrays the Ascension, beside scenes of the Transfiguration and the Baptism. In the summer months, the cathedral courtyard is home to stalls selling local crafts.

MUSÉE DE LA CIVILISATION
(MUSEUM OF CIVILIZATION) ✪

Inaugurated in 1988 and designed by Moshe Safdie, this building is a splendid example of how modern architecture can be integrated into the old city – incorporated within its walls is a four-story stone house, the Maison Estèbe, dating from 1751. The museum is devoted to civilization in the broadest sense of the word, and the exhibitions (which change regularly) may feature life in any part of the world at any time. Among its permanent collection, there are fine examples of Québécois furniture, sculpture and crafts, as well as important Amerindian artifacts.

DID YOU KNOW?

The church of Notre-Dame-des-Victoires was so named to commemorate two occasions when the British tried to capture Québec but were repulsed. In 1690, Admiral Phipps was defeated, and in 1711 Admiral Walker's fleet was shipwrecked in the river. The British totally destroyed the church during the siege of 1759, but it was rebuilt between 1763 and 1766 and still recalls those earlier French victories.

PLACE ROYALE ⊙⊙

This charming square is located in the center of the Basse-Ville (Lower Town) on the site where Samuel de Champlain built his first settlement in 1608. Today, it is lined with tall stone houses of French Regime style, with steeply pitched roofs and high chimneys (note the ladders on the roofs to enable people to climb up and sweep the chimneys). These houses were actually all rebuilt in the 1970s so that the square could take on the look it had at the time of the conquest, before it was blasted to bits by British mortar fire. A bust of King Louis XIV graces the center of the square, a copy of the original erected in 1686 that gave place Royale its name. On the west side stands the little church of Notre-Dame-des-Victoires with its distinctive steeple.

The narrow pedestrian streets around place Royale are perfect for exploration on foot. There are a number of craft stores along rue Petit-Champlain, antiques shops on rue St-Paul, and souvenir outlets just about everywhere.

✚ 44B2
🍴 Restaurants/cafés ($–$$$)
♿ Few
❓ Access from Upper Town by funicular (inexpensive), or by descending the "Breakneck Steps" on foot

Bronze bust of Louis XIV

PROMENADE DES GOUVERNEURS (▶ 25, TOP TEN)

STE-ANNE-DE-BEAUPRÉ ⊙⊙

This small community on the north shore of the St. Lawrence overlooking Île d'Orléans has been a major place of pilgrimage for Roman Catholics since the early 1600s, when Breton sailors were brought safely to land here during a storm after praying to St. Anne. The twin-spired basilica that dominates the site today was inaugurated in 1934. Constructed of white granite in the form of a Latin cross, it has a magnificent interior with five naves, a barrel vault decorated with mosaics, and luminous stained-glass windows. Every year, a million or more pilgrims visit the basilica's north transept to pray before the statue of St. Anne holding the infant Mary. The chapel behind the statue contains a relic of the saint, which was given to the shrine by Pope John XXIII in 1960.

✚ 44B2

Sanctuaire Ste-Anne-de-Beaupré
www.ssadb.qc.ca
✉ 10018 avenue Royale, Ste-Anne-de-Beaupré. . About 35km (22 miles) from Québec City via Highway 40 and Route 138
☎ 418/827-3781
🕐 Daily (phone for times of Mass)
🍴 Cafeteria ($)
♿ Very good 🎫 Free
↔ Chute Montmorency (▶ 55)

TERRASSE DUFFERIN (▶ 25, TOP TEN)

Food & Drink

Atlantic Provinces

Not surprisingly for a region so closely connected with the sea, there is seafood galore here: large, luscious Malpeque

oysters from Prince Edward Island (PEI); tender Digby scallops from Nova Scotia; and fat red lobsters, also from PEI, where attendance at a community lobster supper is de rigueur. In New Brunswick, the Atlantic salmon is wonderful; Oven Head, near St. Andrews-by-the-Sea, is a great place to buy it smoked.

In Newfoundland, fish and brewis (salt codfish and seabiscuit) is a favorite dish, while for dessert you

A tantalizing display of fresh seafood from Nova Scotia

could try figgy duff, a steaming-hot raisin pudding. In the Acadian areas, chicken *fricot* (hearty chicken soup) will warm you up, or try *poutine rappé* (potato dumpling with salt pork).

In Halifax, Alexander Keith's India pale ale is distinctly hoppy in flavor. Drink it with Solomon Grundy (marinated herring – a touch salty), or swig it down with fiddleheads, the tender curled ends of ferns, lightly boiled and slathered in butter. Finish your meal with chocolates from Chocolatier Ganong in St. Stephen, New Brunswick – but don't count the calories.

Below: selection of Québec beers

Québec

There is a small wine industry in southern Québec and a

plethora of microbreweries making beers with such colorful names as Maudite (Damned), Fin du Monde (End of the World) and Eau Bénite (Holy Water). As an aperitif or after-dinner drink, try Sortilège, made from maple syrup and Canadian whisky, or Chicoutai, made from cloudberries.

Right: fiddleheads – unopened fronds of the ostrich fern

The local Camembert and brie cheeses are delicious, especially when eaten with some of the wonderful breads produced by such companies as Montréal's Première Moisson. In Montréal, juicy slices of smoked meat piled high on rye bread is a tradition brought by Jewish settlers from Eastern Europe (► 95). Alternatively, try some *tourtière* (minced meat and potato), and finish with *tarte au sucre* (sugar pie). Again, don't count the calories!

Apples grown in the Rougemont area are used to make alcoholic ciders, apple vinegars and even iced cider. The latter is delicious with foie gras, a side product of the ducks raised around Brome Lake, where thinly sliced *magret de canard* (duck breast) is a specialty. On Île d'Orléans, the Domaine Steinbach is one of several places in Québec making wonderful mustards.

Cabane à sucre *(sugar shack) in Rigaud, west of Montréal*

In spring, a visit to a *cabane à sucre* (sugar shack) is fun. Celebrate the end of winter like a local by pouring maple syrup over everything – ham, beans, eggs, pancakes and so on. Wash it all down with a glass of caribou (a lethal mixture of brandy, vodka, sherry and port) or a kir (white wine and crème de cassis). And don't forget to try some maple taffy – hot maple syrup poured onto the snow and then eaten off a stick.

Popular with Québecois teenagers is a cholesterol-heavy mixture of French fries, cheese curds and gravy known as *poutine*. You can even get the dish at McDonald's, although don't forget to call the food chain "McDoe" here, as the kids do.

Ontario

The Niagara peninsula is a famous wine-making area that is known particularly for its ice wine, made with grapes that have frozen on the vine. It is quite sweet and rather expensive (► 97). There's lots of fresh produce here too – peaches, cherries, apricots and so on – as well as delicious jams.

Toronto boasts excellent restaurants known for their "fusion cuisine," but it's also a mecca for ethnic food from every corner of the world. Try visiting Kensington Market on a Saturday (► 77) or the St. Lawrence Market in Toronto for a peameal bacon sandwich (► 98). Canadian Club Whisky has been made in Walkerville (Windsor) for 150 years. It's lighter than scotch and smoother than bourbon, and it tastes great with a chunk of Canadian cheddar cheese made in Ingersoll.

Walk Around the Québec City Walls

Distance
4.6km (2.8 miles)

Time
About 2 hours

Start/end point
Centre Infotouriste on place
d'Armes opposite Château
Frontenac
✚ 44B2

Lunch
Gambrinus ($$)
✉ 15 rue du Fort (off place
d'Armes)
☎ 418/692-5144

*From the Centre Infotouriste, walk left to
Terrasse Dufferin (➤ 25, Top Ten), and then
alongside it. Cross the bottom of the winter
toboggan slide (right) and take the Escalier de la
Terrasse up to rue St-Denis (65 steps). Climb
another 50 steps up to the Citadel (left).*

From here the view is splendid, and you can look down
into the outer moat of this formidable fortress (➤ 55).

*Follow the star-shape of the Citadel to the right
to the main entrance. Cross Côte de la Citadelle
via the footbridge and bear right along the city
walls. Cross rue St-Louis by the Porte St-Louis.*

This is one of three picturesque gates in the walls, built
between 1878 and 1781. The French Second Empire
building to your left houses the Québec Legislative
Assembly (Assemblée nationale; 1877–86).

Cross rue Dauphine by the Porte Kent.

This gate was named after the Duke of Kent, father of
Queen Victoria and governor general of Canada (1792–94).

Cross rue St-Jean by the Porte St-Jean.

Next to you here inside the walls is Parc de l'Artillerie, an
area once reserved for the manufacture of armaments.

Cross rue Richelieu (still in Parc de l'Artillerie).

Note the Dauphine Redoubt (right), built between 1712
and 1748 and identifiable by its supporting buttresses.

Cross Côte-du-Palais.

The buildings ahead on the right house the Hôtel-Dieu, the
oldest hospital in North America, founded nuns in 1637.

*Continue along rue des Remparts and look
down at the city below (left). The road swings
right, offering a view of the Château Frontenac
ahead. Cross Parc Montmorency, take the
footbridge across Côte de la Montagne and climb
the 83 steps to regain place d'Armes.*

*Horse-drawn calèches
beside Porte St-Louis in
the city walls*

What to See in Québec Province

CHARLEVOIX COAST ✪✪✪
On the north shore of the St. Lawrence River east of Québec City is the Charlevoix coast, where mountains sweep down to the water's edge and charming villages nestle in the valleys. There are ever-changing views of the mighty river and its opposite shore, as well as possibilities for whale-watching (➤ 26, Top Ten). In 1989, the Charlevoix was named a UNESCO World Biosphere Reserve for its unique beauty.

The rocky mountainous landscape of Charlevoix was created about 350 million years ago when a gigantic meteorite hit the Earth, making a crater that stretches some 56km (35 miles) from Baie-St-Paul to La Malbaie. It's the biggest such crater in the world. Highlights of the region include Baie-St-Paul, whose beautiful location among rolling hills in the Gouffre valley has long been a magnet for artists; the rural charm of Île-aux-Coudres; and La Malbaie, known for its resort hotels, including the Manoir Richelieu.

EASTERN TOWNSHIPS (CANTONS DE L'EST) ✪
Settled by Loyalists at the end of the 18th century, the Eastern Townships are a unique mixture of Anglo-Saxon ambience and French *joie de vivre*. They offer mountains rising nearly 1,000m (about 3,000 feet) with a number of ski slopes, lakes perfect for boating and swimming, and quiet villages. Knowlton near Brome Lake is a charming place with a variety of craft stores and restaurants. Magog is superbly set at the northern end of long and narrow Lake Memphrémagog, while the nearby monastery of **St-Benoît-du-Lac**, known for the cheeses made by its monks, has unusual multicolored buildings with steeply pitched roofs and a tall tower.

Abbaye St-Benoît-du-Lac, Eastern Townships

---

www.
tourisme-charlevoix.com

🕂 44B2

🍴 Restaurants in all the main communities ($–$$$)

ℹ️ Association touristique régionale de Charlevoix: 495 boulevard de Comporté, La Malbaie, Québec, G5A 3G3 ☎ 418/665-4454, 800/667-2276 (toll free)

↔️ Whale-watching, Tadoussac (➤ 26, Top Ten)

❓ Ferry from St-Joseph to Île-aux-Coudres daily (free; ☎ 418/438-2743)

🕂 44B1

ℹ️ Tourisme Cantons-de-l'Est: 20 rue Don-Bosco Sud, Sherbrooke, Québec, J1H 1R0 ☎ 819/820-2020, 800/355-5755 (toll free)

Abbaie St-Benoît
www.st-benoit-du-lac.com

✉️ St-Benoît-du-Lac, Québec, J0B 2M0. 14km (9 miles) south of Magog via Route 112 and minor road signed "Abbaie Saint-Benoît"

☎ 819/843-4080

🕐 Monastery: daily. Store: Mon–Sat (closed during the Eucharist). Gregorian chant: at Eucharist daily 11 am; and at Vespers Wed and Fri–Mon 5 pm, Tue and Thu 7 pm, summer; Fri–Wed 5 pm, Thu 7 pm, rest of year

♿ Very good

❓ Respectable clothing required

Drive Along the Gaspé Peninsula

Distance
236km (147 miles)

Time
1 day (at least)

Start point
Grande-Vallée on the north shore (Route 132)
➕ 44B3

End point
Grande-Rivière on the south shore (Route 132)
➕ 44C3

Lunch
Buy a picnic in Gaspé or Percé; numerous picnic places are passed along the route

Forillon National Park
www.parkscanada.gc.ca/forillon
☎ 418/368-5505
🕐 Daily
💰 Moderate May–Oct, free rest of year

The rocky coastline of Forillon National Park

This glorious drive comprise some of the most grandiose landscapes in Québec. Beyond Grande-Vallée, it's one rocky headland after another, with constantly changing views of coves, capes and the ever-present sea. Distances are given from the start of the drive.

From Grande-Vallée, drive along Route 132 to Rivière-au-Renard.

Rivière-au-Renard (64km/40 miles) is the most important fishing community of Gaspésie.

Continue to Cap-des-Rosiers (85km/53 miles).

The lighthouse here is a landmark for miles around.

Immediately after leaving Cap-des-Rosiers, you enter Forillon National Park.

Shaped by erosion, the rugged coastline of Forillon rises above the sea like a massive tilted block. A short detour takes you to the park's interesting Interpretive Centre, where boat cruises leave for close-ups of the cliffs, their colonies of sea birds and seals on the rocks.

The road crosses the Forillon peninsula and then detours around the Baie de Gaspé to cross the Dartmouth River by a long bridge.

The city of Gaspé (127km/79 miles) is set on a hillside sloping down to the York River. The Cathédrale de Christ-Roi, built in 1969, is constructed entirely of wood.

Continue along Route 132.

Beyond Gaspé, there are many wonderful views of the Forillon peninsula to your left, and at Pointe-St-Pierre (175km/109 miles) you get your first view of the site of Percé and its famous rock. Percé (204km/127 miles) is renowned for its beautiful site (► 22, Top Ten). As you leave the town, stop at the viewpoint on Cap Blanc for a view back to Rocher Percé and Mont-Ste-Anne.

Continue to Cap d'Espoir (220km/137 miles), for a last view back towards Percé. The coast now swings steadily to the west. The drive ends at Grande-Rivière (236km/147 miles).

ÎLE D'ANTICOSTI ✪

Once a private hunting and fishing camp, the island of Anticosti in the Gulf of the St. Lawrence is today largely owned by the province of Québec and run as a nature reserve. Île d'Anticosti covers a massive 8,000sq km (3,000 square miles) and has much to offer nature lovers. There are more than 200 bird species (including bald eagles), a herd of white-tailed deer, impressive rock formations, caverns, waterfalls and the remains of about 200 shipwrecks off the rocky shores. Take the 3km (2-mile) hike up a canyon to see Vauréal Falls. Here, the river plunges 76m (249 feet) into the steep-walled canyon.

www.anticosti-ile.com

✚ 44C3

ℹ Municipalité de l'Île d'Anticosti: Box 119, Port-Menier, Québec, G0G 2Y0 ☎ 418/535-0250

🚢 Relais Nordik: ☎ 418/723-8787; **www.desgagnes.com**

✈ Air Satellite: ☎ 418/538-2332; **www.air-satellite.com**

ÎLE D'ORLÉANS ✪✪

The island of Orléans sits wedged like a giant cork in the St. Lawrence River as it widens beyond Québec City. In the early 17th century, French settlers began farming the fertile soil here and built the stone churches and Norman-style farmhouses with steeply pitched roofs that still grace its shores. In the summer months, the island becomes a vast open-air market, with fruit and vegetables on sale at roadside stands; it is especially famous for its strawberries.

Route 368 makes a circular tour (about 70km/45 miles) of Île d'Orléans, giving some wonderful views of the tide-swept shores of the St. Lawrence and of Québec City. You will pass, and can visit, the **Manoir Mauvide-Genest**, a French manor house built in 1734 that has been splendidly restored. The small stone church of St-Pierre, built between 1717 and 1719, is no longer consecrated but it offers a veritable museum of religious art. The island also has some excellent restaurants.

✚ 44B2

ℹ Chambre de commerce de l'Île d'Orléans: 490 côte du Pont, St-Pierre-de-l'Île d'Orléans, Québec, G04 4E0 ☎ 418/828-9411

Manoir Mauvide-Genest

✉ 1451 chemin Royal, St-Jean, Québec, G0A 3W0

☎ 418/829-2630

🕐 Daily, Jun–early Sep; Sat–Sun, rest of year

♿ Good

✋ Moderate

Église St-Pierre

✉ 1249 chemin Royale, St-Pierre-de-l'Île d'Orléans, Québec, G0A 4E0

☎ 418/828-9824

🕐 Daily, May–Oct

♿ Few

✋ Free

Inside the restored Manoir Mauvide-Genest, St.-Jean

+ 44A2

Musée Louis-Hémon
www.destination.ca/museelh
✉ 700 route Maria
   Chapdelaine, Péribonka,
   Québec, G0W 2G0
☎ 418/374-2177
🕐 Daily, May–Oct; Sat–Sun,
   rest of year
♿ Good 🎫 Moderate

Village historique de Val-Jalbert
www.sepaq.com
✉ Route 169, Chambord,
   Québec, G0W 1G0
☎ 418/275-3132
🕐 Daily, mid-May to mid-Oct
♿ Few 🎫 Expensive

+ 44A1

Croisières Alouette
www.canada-laurentides.com
(in French)
✉ Ste-Agathe-des-Monts,
   Québec, J8C 3A3
☎ 819/326-3656
🕐 Daily, mid-May to Oct
♿ Few
🎫 Expensive

Tremblant
www.tremblant.ca
✉ 1000 chemin des
   Voyageurs, Mont-
   Tremblant, Québec, J8E
   1T1. 96km (60 miles)
   northwest of Montréal via
   Highway 15, Route 117,
   and Route 327
☎ 800/857-8043 (toll-free)
🕐 Daily
🍴 Restaurants and cafés
   ($$–$$$)
♿ Few

Pedestrian streets at the heart of the Tremblant resort

LAC ST-JEAN

Located north of Québec City, this large, saucer-shaped lake (1,350sq km/521 square miles) is the source of the Saguenay River (► 65). The land around is flat and fertile, and is particularly known for the wild blueberries (*bleuets*) that grow on its northern shore. In the water, a species of lake trout known as ouananiche flourishes, highly prized by sports fishermen. Lac St-Jean is renowned in the French-speaking world as the setting for *Maria Chapdelaine*, probably the most famous novel of French Canada ever written. In Péribonka, you can learn all about this beautiful love story at the **Musée Louis-Hémon**.

Splendidly set beside Ouiatchouan Falls, the former mill town of Val-Jalbert evokes the hopes and dreams of another age. It has now been partially restored, and you can walk its deserted streets and look at the abandoned homes. Don't miss climbing to the top of the falls (via 400 steps or a cable-car ride) for the view over the lake.

LAURENTIANS (LES LAURENTIDES) ⭐⭐

When Montréalers talk of the "Laurentides," they are referring to the mountains just north of the city where ski centers and lakes abound, and to which half the population retreats on weekends. This is a land of sport, leisure, good food and *joie de vivre*. Surrounded by mountains and famous for its restaurants is St-Sauveur-des-Monts, the region's oldest resort. At Ste-Agathe-des-Monts, you can take a boat trip around lovely Lac-des-Sables (Sandy Lake). The vast **Tremblant complex**, meanwhile, is an astounding place surrounded by wilderness; the buildings, with their steeply pitched red and blue roofs, house boutiques, restaurants, bars and accommodations of every type. Considered the top ski resort in eastern North America, Tremblant has plenty to offer year-round.

SAGUENAY FJORD ⭐⭐⭐

For the final 60km (37 miles) before it joins the St. Lawrence, the Saguenay River passes through a deep channel in the rock gouged out by glaciers millions of years ago. Precipitous cliffs rise 500m (1,600 feet) above dark waters that plunge to 240m (787 feet). This stark landscape, where the hand of man is barely visible, is best appreciated by taking a boat trip. One highlight of the tour is Cap Trinité, so named for the three ledges that punctuate its face. On the first of these is a 9m-high (30-foot) statue of the Virgin carved in 1881, an awe-inspiring sight. There are also a few viewpoints of the fjord from Routes 170 and 172, and at Rivière-Éternité you can follow a steep trail up to the statue of the Virgin (allow four hours return).

TADOUSSAC WHALE-WATCHING CRUISES
(► 26, TOP TEN)

TROIS-RIVIÈRES ⭐

An industrial center known for its pulp and paper mills, Trois-Rivières is the third city of Québec province. As it joins the St. Lawrence here, the St. Maurice River branches around two islands – hence the name Trois-Rivières (Three Rivers). Close to the river, rue des Ursulines has some of the oldest-surviving buildings in the community, the most striking of which is the domed Monastère des Ursulines (Ursuline Convent) of 1697. Nearby, a waterfront promenade offers views of the port and the Laviolette Bridge across the St. Lawrence. In neighboring Cap-de-la-Madeleine is the **Sanctuaire Notre-Dame-du-Cap**, a magnificent octagonal basilica (inaugurated in 1964). The church forms part of a shrine devoted to the Virgin that is visited by half a million pilgrims every year.

🔲 44B2

🚢 Croisières La Marjolaine: Chicoutimi (418/543-7630, 800/363-7248 toll-free). Croisières AML: Tadoussac and Baie-Ste-Catherine ☎ 418/692-1159, 800/563-4643 (toll-free). Tours Dufour, Richelieu, Saguenay ☎ 418/692-0222, 800/463-5250 (toll-free). All boat tours run daily, late Jun–Sep; very expensive; reservations essential

🕐 Rivière-Éternité walk: daily, mid-May to mid-Oct

🅿 Parking at Rivière-Éternité: expensive

🔲 44A1

Sanctuaire Notre-Dame-du-Cap

www.sanctuaire-ndc.ca

✉ 626 rue Notre-Dame, Cap-de-la-Madeleine, Québec, G8T 4G9

☎ 819/374-2441

🕐 Daily 🍴 Cafeteria ($)

♿ Excellent 🅿 Free

❓ Phone for times of English Masses

Above: *Mist over Rivière Ste.-Marguerite, on Saguenay Fjord*

Ontario

Ontario is Canada's heartland economically, politically and culturally; it is also the most populous of all the provinces and the richest. The waters of four of the five Great Lakes wash its shores and it takes its name from one of them. In fact, the word Ontario actually means "shining waters," an apt description of a province that includes 200,000sq km (70,000 square miles) of lakes. The beauty of such natural regions as the Thousand Islands and Georgian Bay is closely associated with water, and Ontario's major cities are all located either beside a lake or large river. Thunder Bay lies on Lake Superior, Sault Ste. Marie is on the St. Mary's River, Ottawa has an impressive site on the river of the same name, and Toronto – the province's capital, largest city and financial center – sits majestically on the northern shore of Lake Ontario. Last but not least, the province boasts the magnificent spectacle of Niagara Falls, one of the world's great tourist attractions.

> *' See all its store of inland waters hurl'd*
> *In one vast volume down Niagara's steep;*
> *Or calm behold them, in transparent sleep,*
> *Where the blue hills of old Toronto shed*
> *Their evening shadows o'er Ontario's bed. '*

Tom Moore
From "To the Lady Charlotte Rawdon," *Poetical Works* (1804)

View from Thousands Islands Parkway

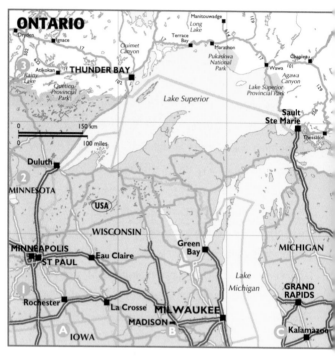

69F3

National Capital
Commission Infocentre
www.canadascapital.gc.ca

✉ 90 Wellington Street
(opposite Parliament
Buildings), Ottawa,
Ontario, K1P 5A1

☎ 613/239-5000, 800/465-
1867 (toll-free)

🕐 Daily

Ottawa ✪✪✪

As befits a nation's capital, Ottawa has its fair
share of imposing architecture: The Parliament
Buildings are a masterpiece of Gothic fantasy and
some of the national museums are splendidly
housed. But visitors tend to remember the
beautiful drives by the river, the canal (which
becomes a vast skating rink in the winter), the
tulips in May and the stalls of fresh produce at the
Byward Market.

Ottawa wasn't originally intended to be the capital. It
started life as a raucous lumber town and was taken over
by the military when the Rideau Canal was built in the
1820s. Queen Victoria considered both Montréal and York
(now Toronto) too close to the U.S. border to be the new
capital of her colony, so in 1857 she chose "Bytown"
instead. This choice did not please everyone, and the city

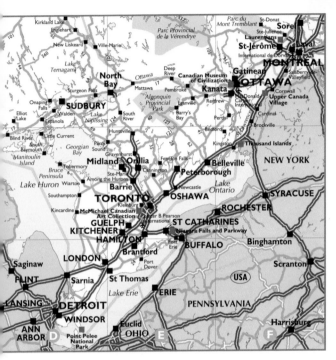

was soon nicknamed "Westminster in the Wilderness" by its detractors. The inhabitants, however, renamed their home after the river on which it stands, thinking it more appropriate for a capital city. And since the Ottawa River marks the boundary between the provinces of Ontario and Québec, between English-speaking and French-speaking Canada, it did indeed prove to be a good choice.

Today, Ottawa is very much a city of government, and is not ruled by the temples of finance as are Toronto and Montréal. Instead, the highrise buildings contain government departments and some of the most expensive homes are owned by civil servants. But Ottawa is not a contrived place created to impress people with the greatness of Canada. In many ways, it defies the image many people have of what a capital city ought to be. It is in the end quintessentially Canadian, and herein lies its charm.

Centre Block on Parliament Hill

What to See in Ottawa

CANADA AVIATION MUSEUM

www.aviation.nmstc.ca
- 69F3
- 11 Aviation Parkway
- 613/993-2010, 800/463-2038 (toll-free)
- Daily 9–5, May–Aug; Wed–Sun 10–5, rest of year
- Cafeteria ($)
- Very good
- Moderate; free Thu 5–9 pm. Parking: free
- Aeronautica gift shop

Housed in a huge triangular hangar, the Canada Aviation Museum is home to a splendid collection of aircraft that illustrate the story of aeronautical history from the first attempts at flight to the jet age. Many deem it to be the most impressive collection of vintage aircraft in the world, which is not too surprising when one considers how important airplanes have been in opening up Canada. Today, Canadian planes and designs are used in rugged terrain worldwide.

The Walkway of Time takes you on a journey through the different eras of aviation development. You can relive the adventures of Canada's bush pilots and see examples of the De Havilland Beaver (this plane was the prototype of a total of 1,600 that were built), and the Twin Otter, two of Canada's most important contributions to international aviation. You can even venture on a virtual-reality hang glider!

CANADA SCIENCE AND TECHNOLOGY MUSEUM

www.science-tech.nmstc.ca
- 69F3
- 1867 St. Laurent Boulevard
- 613/991-3044
- Daily 9–5, May–Aug; Tue–Sun, rest of year
- Very good
- Moderate; additional charge for the Simex Virtual Voyages™ Simulator

This fascinating museum is devoted to the ingenuity of Canadian inventions, and every aspect of the scientific spectrum is featured – from the snowmobile to the Canadarm (part of the space shuttle). With its profusion of waterways, Canada was largely explored by canoe, and the museum has an excellent display detailing the development of this mode of transportation. The Locomotive Hall is another highlight, with an incredible display of huge and powerful locomotives. There's a splendid account of Canada in space, which features a popular Simex Virtual Voyages™ Simulator. In it you can "travel" to Mars to save a colony whose generator has been struck down by a shower of meteorites.

Statuary in the cool Water Court of the National Gallery

70

Tom Thomson, *The Jack Pine*, winter 1916–1917. Oil on canvas. 127.9 x 139.8 cm. National Gallery of Canada, Ottawa.

CANADIAN MUSEUM OF CIVILIZATION (▶ 16, TOP TEN)

CANADIAN WAR MUSEUM ⚫⚫

From the early days of New France through two world wars to present-day peacekeeping duties for the United Nations, Canada has had an interesting military history. This is splendidly brought to life at the Canadian War Museum through the use of life-size dioramas and displays, and by an admirable collection of war art. Highlights include memorabilia from the Battle of Vimy Ridge in 1917, the D-Day landings of 1944 (including a Mercedes-Benz car used by Adolf Hitler), and Korea in the 1950s. A more modern acquisition is the Iltis jeep used by Canadian peacekeepers wounded in Bosnia. In 2005 the Canadian War Museum moves to a new location beside the Ottawa River, with almost double the exhibition space.

www.warmuseum.ca
✚ 69F3
✉ 330 Sussex Drive. From May 2005: 1 Vimy Place
☎ 819/776-8600, 800/555-5621 (toll-free)
🕐 Tue–Sun. The museum will close between Sep 2004 and May 2005 for the move
♿ Very good
💲 Moderate; half-price Sun; free Thu 4–9
❓ Gift store

NATIONAL GALLERY OF CANADA ⚫⚫⚫

Masterpiece of architect Moshe Safdie, the National Gallery of Canada is a visually stunning building with a tower whose glittering prisms echo the Gothic turrets of the Parliamentary Library across the Rideau Canal. It occupies a splendid site in the heart of the city with wonderful views of the Canadian Parliament. Inside, the Great Hall has more splendid views, and the long, elegant galleries, courtyards and skylights diffuse natural light throughout the building.

The gallery is home to more than 1,500 works of Canadian art, from the religious works of New France to today's contemporary presentations. Don't miss the Rideau Chapel, which has a neo-Gothic fan-vaulted ceiling; the Croscup Room, with naive murals painted in Nova Scotia; and the rooms of Inuit art that are hidden away in the basement. The gallery also has an important European collection and hosts major temporary exhibitions.

www.national.gallery.ca
✚ 69F3
✉ 380 Sussex Drive
☎ 613/990-1985, 800/319-2787 (toll-free)
🕐 Daily 10–5 (until 8 pm Thu), May–Sep; Wed–Sun, rest of year
🍴 Restaurant ($$), cafeteria ($)
♿ Very good
💲 Permanent collection: free. Special exhibitions: expensive. On-site pay parking
🔁 Parliament Hill (▶ 72)
❓ Guided tours. Bookstore

www.canadascapital.gc.ca

69F3

Daily

National Capital Commission Infocentre: 90 Wellington Street (opposite Parliament Buildings) ☎ 613/239-5000; 800/465-1867 (toll-free)

Very good

Free

Guided tours leave from Info-Tent daily, 9–5, mid-May to late Jun; 9–8, late Jun–early Sep; from basement of Centre Block rest of year. Changing of the Guard: daily 10 am, late Jun–late Aug. Sound and light shows: daily, late Jun–late Aug ☎ 613/239-5000 for times and language

PARLIAMENT HILL ✪✪✪

The three buildings of the Canadian Parliament stand on a high bluff above the Ottawa River and are commonly referred to as Parliament Hill. Neo-Gothic in their architectural inspiration, their copper roofs, carved stonework, turrets and towers are nothing if not picturesque. The East and West blocks (which house offices) date from the 1860s, while the Centre Block (which houses the House of Commons and the Senate) was rebuilt after a fire in 1916. At the center of the latter is the Peace Tower, 91m (300 feet) high and added in 1927 as a monument to Canadians killed during World War I; it contains a carillon of 53 bells.

The Rideau Canal cuts through the heart of Ottawa

From Wellington Street, walk around the exterior of the buildings (you will pass the Info-Tent, where tours of the interior start in summer). There are wonderful views of the Ottawa River and Gatineau, Québec, as well as monuments to Canadian politicians. Overlooking the river is the Gothic structure that houses the Parliamentary Library, the only part of the Centre Block to survive the 1916 fire.

RIDEAU CANAL AND LOCKS ★

Today, this canal – built in the 1820s as a military route between Ottawa and Kingston (► 84) – forms an attractive linear park as it cuts across the capital. You can stroll or join the joggers beside it, or take a boat cruise along it. In the winter months, it becomes a 7.8km-long (4.8-mile) skating rink. Between Parliament Hill and the Château Laurier Hotel, the canal descends to the Ottawa River via a series of eight flight locks. In the shadow of serious parliamentary business, it's diverting to watch the pleasure craft cruising up and down.

www.canadascapital.gc.ca
🔲 69F3
ℹ️ National Capital Commission Infocentre: 90 Wellington Street (opposite Parliament Buildings) ☎ 613/239-5000; 800/465-1867 (toll free)
♿ Few
❓ Boat cruises (expensive) run daily, mid-May to mid-Oct ☎ 613/225-6781

www.torontotourism.com
69E2

Tourism Toronto
207 Queens Quay West,
Toronto, Ontario, M5J
1A7
416/203-2600
Mon–Fri during business
hours

Toronto

Set on the north shore of Lake Ontario, and with a skyline dominated by the CN Tower, Toronto is an amazingly diverse city. It is a great North American metropolis, vastly wealthy and powerful in financial terms, with a population that is both eclectic and ethnically mixed. There are districts where you are transported to China, Laos or India; to Italy, Portugal or Greece; to Poland, Hungary or Ukraine; and to Chile, San Salvador or Jamaica.

In 1793, Governor John Graves Simcoe decided to locate the new capital of Upper Canada on a swampy site north of Lake Ontario. He called it York after one of the sons of George III, but it was soon nicknamed "Muddy York" because of the state of its streets. In 1813, the Americans burned it to the ground, but it rose from the ashes to become, by the end of the 19th century, a bastion of Anglo-Saxon rectitude. By the 1920s, it was known as "Toronto the Good" and prohibition reigned.

After World War II, the Ontario capital slowly started to blossom. Immigrants poured in from every corner of the world, providing a stimulating mix of social activities and making it one of the world's most ethnically varied cities. Gradually, Toronto took over from Montréal as Canada's economic heart. In the downtown area close to the lake, the country's great fiscal institutions have vied to build bigger and more impressively than one another. As a result, modern-day Toronto boasts an attractive skyline and some spectacular contemporary architecture. It offers a range of interesting attractions for the visitor, including some innovative cultural institutions housing collections to rival those of the world's great museums.

*Toronto's impressive
skyline seen from Lake
Ontario*

What to See in Toronto

ART GALLERY OF ONTARIO ✪✪✪

In 1909, the Art Gallery of Ontario (AGO) started life in The Grange, a Georgian house that is now completely engulfed by the institution. Today, the AGO is one of the best regarded art museums on the continent. It includes a comprehensive installation of Canadian art in a historic context and a European collection strong on the Impressionists. In 2002, Lord Thomson donated his entire collection to the AGO. Once the greatest art collection in private hands in Canada, it includes rare European art objects and works by such masters as Peter Paul Rubens.

No visit to the AGO would be complete without a look at the Henry Moore Sculpture Centre, which houses the world's largest public collection of the works of the great British sculptor. There are a total of 900 bronzes, plasters, maquettes, woodcuts, sketches and etchings, many donated by Moore and located in a beautiful gallery designed by the artist himself.

www.ago.net
🗺 69E2
✉ 317 Dundas Street West
☎ 416/979-6648
🕐 Tue–Sun
🍴 Agora restaurant ($$), cafeteria ($)
Ⓜ St. Patrick
🚊 Dundas streetcar 505
♿ Excellent
💲 Expensive; free Wed 6–8:30 pm
❓ Gallery Shop. Metered street parking. A major expansion project is underway to build galleries to house the Thomson Collection

CN TOWER (▶ 17, TOP TEN)

HARBOURFRONT CENTRE ✪✪

Over the past 30 years, the city's industrial docklands have been renovated to create a recreational and cultural attraction that draws hundreds of thousands of visitors every year. Part of Harbourfront's popularity lies in the infinite variety of the things it offers and the fact that it means different things to different people. Some go there just to wander along the waterfront and to admire the splendid views; others go to shop at Queens Quay Terminal, with its chic stores, or to eat at one of the restaurants there. Some head for York Quay Terminal, with studios housing craftsmen at work; still others take part in one of the large number of events held here, including music and dance performances, art exhibitions, ethnic festivals and literary readings.

www.harbourfront.on.ca
🗺 69E2
✉ South of Queens Quay between York Street and Spadina Avenue
☎ 416/973-4000
🕐 Daily
🍴 Restaurants and cafés ($–$$$)
Ⓜ Union
🚊 Harbourfront streetcar 509, 510
♿ Good
💲 Free. Parking: expensive

75

A Walk Through the Heart of Toronto

Distance
4.8km (3 miles)

Time
2–2.5 hours, excluding visits

Start/end point
Nathan Phillips Square, in
front of Toronto City Hall,
Queen Street West
✚ 69E2
Ⓠ Queen, Osgoode

Lunch
Pumpernickel's Deli ($$)
✉ Queens Quay Terminal
☎ 416/861-0226

*The stunning architecture
of BCE Place*

*Start at City Hall. Cross Bay Street, then take
Albert Street and enter the Eaton Centre, with
its impressive atrium. Exit on Yonge Street and
turn right. Turn left at King Street.*

To your right is Scotia Plaza, across the street is
Commerce Court (Canadian Imperial Bank of Commerce),
ahead First Canadian Place and Toronto-Dominion Centre.

Turn left on Bay Street; cross Wellington Street.

To your right on Bay, the triangular gold-sheathed towers
house the Royal Bank of Canada.

Mid–block enter BCE Place (left).

This elegant galleria, five floors high, incorporates two
older buildings and two unusually shaped office towers.

*Follow Bay Street past Union Station and
under the railroad tracks. Continue under the
Gardiner Expressway to the waterfront. Turn
right and follow the pathway around York
Street slip to Queens Quay Terminal.*

Queens Quay Terminal (➤ 105) houses more than 30
classy stores, galleries and restaurants.

*Follow York Street and the Teamway covered
sidewalk back under the expressway and
railroad. Cross Front Street and turn right at
Wellington Street.*

On both sides are the black-glass buildings of the Toronto-
Dominion Centre.

*Enter the Maritime Life Tower (right), with
its wonderful Inuit art. Cross Wellington Street,
and walk into the courtyard of the TD Centre.*

Life-size bronze cows sit chewing the cud, the work of
Saskatchewan sculptor Joe Fafard.

*Cross King Street and enter First Canadian
Place. Descend by escalator into the PATH
(➤ opposite). Follow signs back to City Hall.*

DID YOU KNOW?

Toronto has a subterranean complex of corridors and walkways, known as the PATH, which connects about 50 of the major buildings of the business district. Lined with stores and food counters, it extends for approximately 12km (7 miles). The underground routes are indicated by the sign "PATH" in colored capitals, followed by directions, so as long as you know where you're going, the network is not complicated to use.

KENSINGTON MARKET ☺☺

The warren of small streets around Kensington Avenue offers an amazing potpourri of businesses. In no other area of Toronto are the city's countless cultures so unceremoniously mixed together. Houses have been converted into shops, and casual restaurants and stores spill out onto the street. Chilean butchers, Italian fishmongers and Portuguese spice merchants stand cheek by jowl with Jamaican fast-food stands and Laotian eateries. You can buy exotic spices, unusual vegetables, fish, cheeses and breads. With its incredible cacophony of sounds it may seem chaotic, but if you want to buy carpets, secondhand furniture or vintage clothing, there's no place like it. Go on a Saturday when the crowd is dense – unless you want to shop seriously, in which case go any day but Saturday.

🚹 69E2
✉ North of Dundas Street West and west of Spadina Avenue
🕐 Daily
🍴 Variety of eateries ($–$$)
🚇 St. Patrick
🚍 Dundas streetcar 505 west
♿ Few

METRO TORONTO ZOO ☺☺

This is not a zoo in the traditional sense of the word. Covering 287 hectares (710 acres), it allows visitors to see animals from different areas of the world in settings that are as natural as possible. The African Savanna reserve is home to elephants, giraffes, antelopes and white rhinos, while a troop of gorillas provides constant entertainment in a separate pavilion. Kangaroos, wombats and pythons star in the Australasian enclosure, and in the Indomalayan pavilion is a tropical forest alive with exotic birds and an orangutan family. In the Eurasian area, camels are the main attraction, although you can also see Siberian tigers, snow leopards, reindeer and yaks. The Canadian Domain re-creates the rugged beauty of the Canadian wilderness with deer, moose, elk and grizzly bears; and the Americas pavilion offers playful otters and a beaver lodge.

www.torontozoo.com
🚹 69E2
✉ Meadowvale Road, Scarborough
☎ 416/392-5900
🕐 Daily; closed Dec 25
🍴 Fast food ($), picnic sites
🚇 Kennedy then bus 86A; Sheppard then bus 85 or 85B
♿ Very good
💲 Very expensive. Parking charge Mar–Oct
❓ Zoomobile mini-train service around the zoo. Large animal-oriented gift store

A baboon – one of the residents of the zoo's Africa pavilion

77

www.ontarioplace.com

✛ 69E2

✉ 955 Lakeshore Boulevard West

☎ 416/314-9900, 866/663-4386 (toll-free)

🕐 Daily, Jun–Aug; some weekends, May and Oct. Cinesphere, Molson Amphitheatre and Atlantis Pavilions: daily

🍴 Restaurants ($–$$)

🚇 Union then free shuttle bus

♿ Good

💲 Very expensive, parking charges

www.ontariosciencecentre.ca

✛ 69E2

✉ 770 Don Mills Road

☎ 416/696-3127. OMNIMAX: 416/696-1000

🕐 Daily; closed Dec 25

🍴 Galileo's Bistro restaurant ($$–$$$), Valley Marketplace cafeteria ($)

🚇 Eglinton, then Eglinton bus 34 east

♿ Very good

💲 Expensive

❓ Mastermind gift store

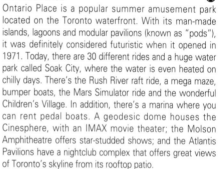

Above: the geodesic dome at Ontario Place

ONTARIO PLACE ✪

Ontario Place is a popular summer amusement park located on the Toronto waterfront. With its man-made islands, lagoons and modular pavilions (known as "pods"), it was definitely considered futuristic when it opened in 1971. Today, there are 30 different rides and a huge water park called Soak City, where the water is even heated on chilly days. There's the Rush River raft ride, a mega maze, bumper boats, the Mars Simulator ride and the wonderful Children's Village. In addition, there's a marina where you can rent pedal boats. A geodesic dome houses the Cinesphere, with an IMAX movie theater; the Molson Amphitheatre offers star-studded shows; and the Atlantis Pavilions have a nightclub complex that offers great views of Toronto's skyline from its rooftop patio.

ONTARIO SCIENCE CENTRE ✪✪

With its 13 exhibition halls, hands-on demonstrations and high-tech, interactive exhibits, this technical extravaganza has to be seen to be believed. Designed by Raymond Moriyama and opened in 1969, the Ontario Science Centre seems to cascade down the Don valley ravine in a series of buildings that stand on different levels and are connected by enclosed escalators. It's the science center to beat all science centers. Want to try navigating on the moon? Then visit the Space Hall. Want to race an Olympic bobsled? Try it out in the Sports Hall. Want to generate your own electricity? Visit the Science Arcade. Want to catch a criminal with DNA fingerprinting? Explore the Human Body exhibit. In case this isn't enough, there's an OMNIMAX theater with a giant 24m (80-foot) wraparound screen where you can have your mind blown away by 13,000 watts of digital sound.

ROYAL ONTARIO MUSEUM ✪✪✪

Far and away Canada's largest museum, the ROM has 40 galleries and 6 million objects of art, archeology and natural science. With something to interest just about everyone, it is justifiably popular. Among the most visited exhibits (especially by children) are the Dinosaur Gallery, where huge skeletons are set in natural habitats, and the Bat Cave, where thousands of lifelike bats swoop and roost in the rocky recesses.

The ROM also has an important collection of Chinese art, including a complete Ming Dynasty tomb, Buddhist wall paintings and sculptures, porcelain, silk robes and objects in jade and ivory. The European galleries have period room displays, the Ancient Egypt gallery features mummies, and the gallery of Earth Sciences has a fabulous collection of gemstones. The Canadiana galleries display decorative arts and historical paintings, and look in detail at the cultures of Canada's indigenous peoples.

Since the ROM first opened its doors in 1914, it has constantly increased in size; at the time of writing, it is undergoing further major expansion, due to be complete in 2005–2006.

www.rom.on.ca
✚ 69E2
✉ 100 Queen's Park
☎ 416/586-5549, 416/586-8000 (24-hour recorded information)
🕐 Daily; closed Dec 25 and Jan 1
🍽 Restaurant ($$$), cafeteria ($)
♿ Museum
🎫 Excellent
💲 Very expensive; free Fri 4:30–9:30 pm
🚇 Yorkville (► 82)
❓ Free guided tours daily. Elaborate gift store selling reproductions

SKYDOME ✪

Situated close to Lake Ontario and the CN Tower, the Toronto SkyDome is a multipurpose mega stadium with a massive domed retractable roof. Used primarily for baseball and football, SkyDome also hosts pop concerts and trade shows. In good weather, the domed roof slides open to expose the entire playing field and most of the stands. There's also a hotel incorporated into the complex, with windows facing onto the field (► 103). Unless you attend an event, the interior can only be viewed by guided tour, which includes a 15-minute film on the construction.

www.skydome.com
✚ 69E2
✉ 1 Blue Jays Way
☎ 416/341-2770 (for tours)
🕐 Guided tours: daily (except during events)
🍽 Fast food ($)
🚇 Union, then 10-minute walk along Skywalk
♿ Few
💲 Guided tours: expensive
🔄 CN Tower (► 17, Top Ten)

Above: *stone warrior outside the Chinese Gallery*

Left: *the SkyDome with its massive retractable roof open*

In the Know

If you only have a short time to visit Eastern Canada, or would like to get a real flavor of the area, here are some ideas:

10 Ways To Be A Local

In Eastern Canada, remember that hockey is a religion – and that it's played on ice.

Wherever you are, remember that Canada is not the 51st state.

In Halifax, stop what you're doing when the noon day gun goes off (➤ 32) and set your watch by it.

In Prince Edward Island, understand that when they talk about the "fixed link," they are referring to Confederation Bridge (➤ 40).

In Newfoundland, practice the art of understatement, and remember that a pond can be a huge lake or deep-sided fjord (➤ 37).

In Montréal, don't look for the sun when given street directions (➤ 48).

In Québec City, don't ask who won the battle on the Plains of Abraham in 1759 (➤ 53).

In Ottawa, photograph a Mountie in red jacket, stetson and boots with spurs, as this is the only place you're likely to see one in ceremonial uniform.

In Toronto, don't ask where the CN Tower is (➤ 17, Top Ten).

In Niagara Falls, unless you want to look out of place, carry a camera and take hundreds of photos.

10 Top Annual Events

Winter Carnival, Québec City: Parade, ice sculptures and canoe races across the ice-strewn St. Lawrence (Feb).

Canadian Tulip Festival, Ottawa: A rite of spring; more than 300,000 tulips decorate the city (May).

Nova Scotia International Tattoo, Halifax: Pipe bands, highland dancers, and military displays for 10 days (Jun–Jul).

Festival 500 – Sharing the Voices, St. John's: International festival of choral singing (Jun–Jul).

International Jazz Festival, Montréal: More than 500 shows, 350 of them outdoors and free, in the heart of downtown (Jun–Jul).

Just for Laughs Comedy Festival, Montréal: 10 days of laughter, with top comedians and free outdoor shows (Jul).

Atlantic Seafood Festival, Moncton, New Brunswick: Top chefs prepare some of the world's best seafood (Aug).

Left: *Just For Laughs Comedy Festival, Montréal*
Below: *International Tattoo, Halifax*

Canadian National Exhibition, Toronto: Huge annual exhibition of just about everything (Aug–Sep).

Oktoberfest, Kitchener, Ontario: Festival of beer, dancing and all things German (Oct).

Christmas Lights Across Canada, Ottawa: Nearly 300,000 lights illuminate the capital to coincide with displays across the country (Dec).

Top Train Excursions

Bras d'Or (Nova Scotia)
☎ 888/842-7245 toll-free (Via Rail) 🕐 Jun–Oct
From Halifax, a 12-hour trip along the shores of lovely Bras d'Or Lake to Sydney in Cape Breton.

Chaleur (Québec)
☎ 888/842-7245 toll-free (VIA Rail) 🕐 Year-round
From Montréal, a splendid 18-hour trip along the shores of the Baie des Chaleurs to Gaspé.

Steam train to Wakefield (Québec)
☎ 819/778-7246 🕐 May to mid-Oct
From Gatineau, a round trip of five hours along the banks of the Gatineau River to the picturesque little village of Wakefield.

Agawa Canyon (Ontario)
☎ 705/946-7300 (Algoma Central) 🕐 Early Jun to mid-Oct
From Sault Ste. Marie, a splendid day trip north through the wilderness of the Canadian Shield with a stop in Agawa Canyon.

Polar Bear Express (Ontario)
☎ 705/472-4500 (Ontario Northland) 🕐 Late Jun–early Sep

From Cochrane, a 12-hour return trip north to Moosonee at Arctic tidewater on the shores of James Bay.

Top Boat Trips

Western Brook Pond (➤ 37).
Bonaventure Island (➤ 22, Top Ten).
Whale-watching off Tadoussac (➤ 26, Top Ten).
Maid of the Mist at Niagara Falls (➤ 20–21, Top Ten).
Thousand Islands (➤ 89).

Good Places to Have Lunch

Cheapside Café ($$)
✉ 1723 Hollis Street, Halifax, Nova Scotia
☎ 902/424-7542
Elegant café in the art gallery offering excellent light lunches and the chance to meet local politicians – the Legislature is across the street.

Restaurant Acadien ($)
✉ 744 Main Street, Chéticamp, Cape Breton, Nova Scotia ☎ 902/224-2170
Charming restaurant in the museum and craft shop serving Acadian specialties; on the Cabot Trail (➤ 39).

Palliser Restaurant ($)
✉ 103–104 Tidal Bore Road, Truro, Nova Scotia
☎ 902/893-8951
Informal restaurant serving seafood, with front-row view of the tidal bore that precedes the changing tide on the Bay of Fundy.

Courtyard Café and Garden ($$)
✉ 145 Richmond Street, Charlottetown, Prince

Edward Island ☎ 902/566-1267
Pleasant café with bistro-style fare in Confederation Centre of the Arts.

Le Café du Château ($)
✉ 280 rue Notre-Dame Est, Montréal, Québec
☎ 514/861-3708
Great salads and light lunches in the Governor's Garden, Château Ramezay Museum, Old Montréal.

Musée Café-Restaurant ($$)
✉ Parc des Champs-de-Bataille, Québec City, Québec ☎ 418/643-2150
Excellent café in the Musée du Québec serving all-Québec produce; outdoor terrace in summer.

Auberge Baker ($$)
✉ 8790 avenue Royale, Château-Richer, Québec
☎ 418/824-4478
Traditional Québec food in a lovely old French house between Québec City and Ste-Anne-de-Beaupré.

Café l'Entrée ($)
✉ 380 Sussex Drive, Ottawa, Ontario
☎ 613/990-1985
Spectacular situation in the Great Hall of the National Gallery of Canada; the menu emphasizes delicious, simply prepared, light foods.

Agora Restaurant ($$)
✉ 317 Dundas Street West, Toronto, Ontario
☎ 416/979-6612
Beautifully located in the glassed-in atrium of the Art Gallery of Ontario; the menu features fresh market flavors and Ontario produce.

Landings Restaurant ($)
✉ 100 Ramsey Lake Road, Sudbury, Ontario
☎ 705/522-0376
Simple, charming restaurant in Science North, overlooking Ramsey Lake.

www.city.toronto.on.ca/parks
🔲 69E2
☎ Toronto Parks: 416/392-1111 (general information); 416/392-8195 (island information line)
🕐 Daily (no winter ferry service to Centre Island)
🍴 Seasonal snack bars ($), picnic sites
🚢 From foot of Bay Street to Hanlan's Point, Centre Island, and Ward's Island ☎ 416/392-8193
♿ Few
🎫 Ferry fare: moderate
❓ Bicycle rentals, public beaches

TORONTO ISLANDS

An urban oasis close to downtown Toronto, these islands consist almost completely of parkland that is closed to motorized traffic. They provide a pleasant retreat from the heat of the city in the summer, as a light refreshing breeze blows in off the lake. For the visitor, they offer absolutely stunning views of the Toronto skyline, as well as beaches, picnic sites, walking and cycling trails, marinas, public moorings, various sporting facilities and the Centreville amusement park for children (▶ 111). The Toronto Islands are actually a series of sand bars composed of material that was eroded from the great bluffs at Scarborough to the east and carried along by lake currents.

Centre Island is the busiest area. From the ferry terminal here, it is about a 45-minute walk to either Hanlan's Point at the western end or to Ward's Island in the east. En route for Hanlan's Point, you will pass the Gibraltar Point Lighthouse. It has a splendid site on Lake Ontario and is reputedly the oldest surviving structure in Toronto (1806).

🔲 69E2
🚇 Bay

YORKVILLE ⭐⭐

With its haute couture boutiques, exclusive galleries, designer stores and pricey restaurants, the area surrounding Yorkville Avenue has become Toronto's most fashionable neighborhood and has some of the most expensive real estate in Canada. However, it was not always this way. Back in the 1960s, Yorkville was the center of the city's counterculture, the hangout of hippies and full of flower children. The rents were low and the drug culture prevailed. But times have changed, and the erstwhile Victorian town houses have been dolled up. Outdoor cafés flourish in the summer months and the tiny laneways connecting Yorkville and Cumberland avenues are chockabloc with the rich and beautiful.

Expensive boutiques and restaurants line Yorkville Avenue

Northern Ontario boasts much wild and rocky scenery

What to See in Ontario

ALGONQUIN PROVINCIAL PARK ✪✪

Covering 7,725sq km (2,983sq miles), Algonquin Provincial Park is the very essence of wilderness. Despite its location in central Ontario within a day's drive of both Ottawa and Toronto, the only way to explore the interior is by canoe or on foot. From the visitor center on Highway 60, a number of trails head for the interior. Algonquin offers splendid opportunities for viewing wildlife. White-tailed deer and bears can be seen, as can moose in spring, early summer and during the mating season in late September. Algonquin is famous for its wolves, which are often heard but only rarely seen – in August, park staff organize "wolf howling" expeditions. More than 260 species of bird have been recorded, including the common loon, which can be found nesting on just about every lake.

www.ontarioparks.com
✚ 69E3
✉ Box 219, Whitney, Ontario, K0J 2M0
☎ 705/633-5572
⊙ Daily
🍴 Food services
💲 Inexpensive
❓ Accommodations available, including campsites

GEORGIAN BAY ✪

Although it is part of Lake Huron, Georgian Bay is almost a lake in its own right thanks to the Bruce Peninsula and Manitoulin Island, which nearly enclose it. The southern part of the bay is blessed with sandy beaches where resorts proliferate. The northern and eastern shorelines are very indented; offshore here are thousands of small rocky islands of smooth granite topped with windswept trees. The wildness of this area has a raw beauty much appreciated by visitors.

The twin harbors at Tobermory, at the tip of the Bruce Peninsula, are full of pleasure craft in the summer months. A ferry crosses from here to Manitoulin Island. Just off Manitoulin is Flowerpot Island, famous for its picturesque sea stacks – visitors can take a cruise around the island and/or land and hike along its coast (4.3km/2.7 miles) to see these rock pillars.

www.tobermory.org
✚ 69D2
ℹ Tobermory Chamber of Commerce: P.O. Box 250, Tobermory, Ontario, N0H 2R0 ☎ 519/596-2452
🚢 Ferry between Tobermory and Manitoulin Island (daily, May–Oct): ☎ 519/596-2510, 800/265-3163 (toll free)
🚤 Access to Flowerpot Island: moderate. Boat cruises: expensive

www.kingstoncanada.com

⊞ 69F2

ℹ Kingston Tourist
Information Office: 209
Ontario Street, Kingston,
Ontario, K7L 2Z1
☎ 613/548-4415,
888/855-4555 (toll-free)

❓ Boats leave Kingston for
the Thousand Islands
(➤ 89)

**Fort Henry National Historic
Site**

www.forthenry.com

✉ P.O. Box 213, Kingston,
Ontario, K7L 4V8

☎ 613/542-7388, 800/437-
2233 (toll free)

🕐 Daily, mid-May to early
Oct

🍴 Soldiers' canteen ($)

♿ Largely accessible

💲 Expensive

↔ Thousand Islands (➤ 89)

❓ Garrison Stores (gift
store); Fort Henry Guard
sunset ceremonies: Wed,
Jul–Aug (phone for details
of other performances)

⊞ 69E2

**McMichael Canadian Art
Collection**

www.mcmichael.com

✉ 10365 Islington Avenue,
Kleinburg, Ontario, L0J
1C0

☎ 905/893-1121, 888/213-
1121 (toll-free)

🕐 Daily; closed Dec 25

🍴 Restaurant ($$)

♿ Excellent

💲 Expensive. Parking
charge

❓ Gallery shop

Right: the McMichael
has a splendid collection
of Inuit art

Opposite: the elegant
main street of Niagara-on-
the-Lake has many fine
19th-century buildings

KINGSTON ✪✪

Located at the eastern end of Lake Ontario, Kingston is a gracious city of limestone buildings and tree-lined streets, home to Queens University and the Royal Military College. Its grandiose City Hall was built in 1844 as a possible Parliament in the days when the city hoped to become the capital of Canada. An important British naval base in the early 19th century, it was equipped with a dockyard and an impressive stone fortress. Today restored to its full splendor, **Fort Henry** offers an excellent picture of military life in the mid-19th century, with barracks, officers' quarters, kitchens, guard room and powder magazine, all animated by costumed interpreters. Don't miss the Fort Henry Guard, a troop of specially recruited and trained students who give high-precision military performances.

> ### DID YOU KNOW?
>
> Every year, the force of the water tumbling over Niagara Falls erodes the rock. In fact, 12,000 years ago, the Horseshoe Falls were 11km (7 miles) downstream at Queenston Heights. Today, the rate of erosion is estimated to be 36cm (1 foot) every 10 years. So, in a few hundred thousand years, the falls will have eroded their way back to Lake Erie and thus cease to exist!

KLEINBURG ✪✪✪

The small community of Kleinburg in the Humber River valley north of Toronto has a splendid **art collection** given to the province of Ontario by Robert and Signe McMichael. Located in a series of sprawling square-hewn log buildings, the gallery is devoted entirely to Canadian art and features the finest collection in existence of works by the Group of Seven. In the 1920s, these artists sought to create a Canadian way of representing their country on its own terms rather than in the European tradition.

The galleries are arranged so that you can just ramble around admiring the works while at the same time looking out of the large windows at scenery similar to that depicted in the canvases. The McMichael also owns a superb collection of First Nations art, including sculptures by West Coast peoples, the striking prints of Norval Morrisseau and Inuit soapstone carvings.

NIAGARA FALLS (▶ 20–21, TOP TEN)

NIAGARA-ON-THE-LAKE

One of the most charming communities in Ontario is set on the shores of Lake Ontario at the mouth of the Niagara River. Settled by Loyalists after the American Revolution, Niagara-on-the-Lake was burned to the ground by the Americans during the War of 1812. It was rebuilt soon afterwards, and today is a quiet town of gracious homes and tree-lined streets far from the bustle and commotion of Niagara Falls. It is also at the center of the flourishing Niagara wine industry (▶ 97).

Niagara-on-the-Lake is renowned for its annual Shaw Festival (▶ 113) and also for **Fort George**. Built in the 1790s, this garrison played an important role in the War of 1812 and has been restored to reflect that time with grassy earthworks and a wooden stockade.

NIAGARA PARKWAY

The Niagara Parkway follows the river of the same name on its course from Lake Erie to Lake Ontario. Put in place in 1923 by the Niagara Parks Commission, the parkway protects the natural environment around Niagara Falls from unbridled commercial development. As a drive, it is interesting because of the variety of scenery it encompasses, including the spectacle of the falls themselves and the immense hydroelectric potential of this roaring water, as well as more tranquil sections with substantial homes, attractive gardens and the **Niagara Parks Botanical Gardens**.

At **Queenston Heights**, the Niagara Parkway crosses the Niagara Escarpment, a massive ridge of sedimentary rock towering 106m (350 feet) above the river. The escarpment provides good soil and protection for the rich farmlands, orchards and vineyards of the area.

69E2
Niagara-on-the-Lake Chamber of Commerce: 26 Queen Street, Niagara-on-the-Lake, Ontario, L0S 1J0 ☎ 905/468-1950

Fort George National Historic Park
www.parkscanada.gc.ca
✉ 26 George Street
☎ 905/468-4257
🕐 Daily 10–5, Apr–Oct
🍴 Restaurants in town ($–$$$)
♿ Good 🎫 Moderate

www.niagaraparks.com
69E2
✉ Niagara Parks Commission: 7400 Portage Road South, Oak Hall Administrative Building, Niagara Falls, Ontario, L2E 6T2 (☎ 905/356-2241)

Queenston Heights Park and Niagara Parks Botanical Gardens
☎ 905/371-0254
🕐 Daily
🚌 Niagara People Mover bus (Mar–Dec)
♿ Good 🎫 Free

Drive Along the Niagara Parkway

The Niagara Parkway begins at the Mather Arch, a gateway for travelers entering Canada over the Peace Bridge, which connects Fort Erie with Buffalo, New York state. Distances are given from the start of the drive, except where stated.

After 6km (4 miles), the river widens and flows around Grand Island. Beyond here, the Niagara Parkway passes through Chippawa (24km/15 miles) and Dufferin Islands Park.

In the river, hydroelectric installations can be seen where the water diverts to power stations downstream. The river moves nearly 100kph (60mph) through great rapids here.

At the 28km (17-mile) point, you reach Table Rock and Horseshoe Falls, followed by American Falls and the Maid of the Mist *(➤ 20–21, Top Ten). Beyond the falls, you pass under two bridges; stop at the second (32km/20 miles).*

The Great Gorge Adventure is an elevator ride to the bottom of the gorge, where you can view the impressive rapids created below the falls. Across the street is the Ten Thousand Buddhas Sarira Stupa.

Continue for a further kilometer (0.6 mile).

An impressive whirlpool here is created by the force and speed of the water; the cable car suspended high above it offers thrilling views.

After 37km (23 miles), you pass the Niagara Parks Botanical Gardens (➤ 85), then drive over the top of the Adam Beck Generating Station.

On the far bank, the Robert Moses Generating Station serves the U.S. side of the river.

Continue to Queenston Heights Park (40km/ 25 miles; ➤ 85), with its monument commemorating the War of 1812. From here, the Niagara Parkway descends the Niagara Escarpment and bypasses the village of Queenston to reach Niagara-on-the-Lake.

Distance
52km (32 miles)

Time
Allow half a day

Start point
Mather Arch, Fort Erie
🚇 69E2

End point
Niagara-on-the-Lake
🚇 69E2

Lunch
Queenston Heights
Restaurant ($$)
✉ 14184 Niagara Parkway
☎ 905/262-4274

Great Gorge Adventure
4330 River Road
☎ 905/374-1221
🕐 Daily, Apr–Oct
🚌 Niagara People Mover bus (Mar–Dec)
♿ Few
💲 Moderate

Niagara Spanish Aero Car
✉ 3850 Niagara Parkway
☎ 905/371-0254,
🕐 Daily, Apr–Feb

Opposite and above: *the historic Spanish aero car gives outstanding views of the Whirlpool Rapids*

www.parkscanada.gc.ca
🔶 69D1
✉ 407 Monarch Lane, RR1
Leamington, Ontario,
N8H 3V4
☎ 519/322-2365, 519/322-
2371 (recorded message)
🅒 Daily
🍴 Cattail Café on the marsh
boardwalk
♿ Good
💰 Moderate
❓ Tip of Canadian mainland
accessible by private
vehicle Nov–Mar; by free
shuttle bus Apr–Oct.
Bookstore in visitor
center

POINT PELEE NATIONAL PARK

At 42 degrees north (the same latitude as northern California, Rome and Sapporo, Japan), Point Pelee has a plant and animal life unique in Canada. This triangular peninsula in Lake Erie is what is known as a "migration trap," a place that attracts birds from a wide variety of species. And during the spring and fall migrations, literally thousands of them pass through, giving Point Pelee an impressive checklist of more than 350 species. At these times, seeing 100 species a day is not unusual for experienced birders. Visitors are also drawn to Point Pelee to view the quite remarkable fall migration of the monarch butterfly. The Park Visitor Centre offers a wealth of information. However, no visit to Point Pelee would be complete without a trek to the most southerly tip of the Canadian mainland, where a covered exhibit area provides information on bird migration. There's also a boardwalk through Point Pelee's marsh, where observation towers offer great views.

www.
city.sault-ste-marie.on.ca
🔶 68C2
✉ Corporation of the City of
Sault Ste. Marie: 99
Foster Drive, Sault Ste.
Marie, Ontario, P6A 5X6
☎ 705/759-2500

**Lock Tours Canada Boat
Cruises**
www.locktours.com
✉ Roberta Bondar Park,
Sault Ste. Marie
☎ 705/253-9850, 877/226-
3665 (toll free)
🅒 Daily, mid-May to mid-
Oct
💰 Expensive

SAULT STE. MARIE

The "Soo" is located on the north side of the St. Mary's River, which connects Lake Superior to Lake Huron. In just 1.5km (1 mile), this river drops more than 6m (21 feet) in a string of turbulent rapids (*sault* in French). Today, one of the busiest canal systems in the world is in place here, incorporating some of the world's longest locks (411m/ 1,350 feet) so that shipping can make the passage. Boat cruises offer visitors the chance of viewing this last stage of the St. Lawrence Seaway, where ships complete their journey from the Atlantic into the heart of the continent. The Algoma railroad offers day trips into the wilderness to the north of Sault Ste. Marie (▶ 81).

*Boardwalks cross the
marshes in Point Pelee
National Park*

Sudbury's Big Nickel stands 9m (30 feet high)

SUDBURY ⭐⭐

Sudbury sits on the largest-known source of nickel and copper ores in the world. First and foremost a mining and refining center, it is dominated by a 380m-high (1,250-foot) chimney, known as "Super Stack." Most people make the trek to Sudbury to visit Science North (► 23, Top Ten), but there is also a fascinating mine to see here.

Dynamic Earth is housed in the former Big Nickel Mine. An elevator transports you to the bottom of a rock chasm cut 20m (65 feet) down into the rock. As you descend, you view a multimedia presentation projected onto the rock face. Then, as you tour the mine, you encounter former miners acting the roles of characters from Sudbury's mining history. Back at the surface, an exhibition center explains the geological importance of the crater in which Sudbury is located.

THOUSAND ISLANDS ⭐⭐

As it leaves Lake Ontario, the St. Lawrence River passes a multitude of islands of different sizes, some large and forested, others simply rocky outcrops supporting a few pine trees. The exposed bedrock here is Precambrian granite, which has a pinkish hue in places. This rock, combined with the sparkling waters and the surrounding greenery, makes the Thousand Island region delightful.

To experience the area to the full, you should take a boat trip. The variety of summer homes you will see is as great as the number of islands: There are large, luxurious mansions, elegant wood-framed structures, vacation cabins, chalets and simple shacks. Some boat trips stop to visit the amazing six-story extravaganza on tiny Heart Island, built between 1900 and 1904 by George C. Boldt.

---

www.
city.greatersudbury.on.ca
🚩 69D3
✉ City of Greater Sudbury: Station A, 200 Brady Street, Sudbury, Ontario, P3A 5P3 ☎ 705/671-2489, ext. 4611

Dynamic Earth
www.dynamicearth.ca
✉ 122 Big Nickel Road
☎ 705/522-3701
🕐 Daily, May–Oct
♿ Good
🎫 Very expensive

---

www.
1000islandsgananoque.com
🚩 69F2
🚢 Boat tours to Thousand Islands (expensive) run daily, May–Oct.
Gananoque Boat Line: 6 Water Street, Gananoque ☎ 613/382-2144.
Rockport Boat Line Ltd.: 23 Front Street, Rockport ☎ 613/659-3402.
Kingston 1000 Islands Cruises: 263 Ontario Street, Kingston ☎ 613/549-5544

www.thunderbay.ca
 68B3
ℹ Thunder Bay Economic
Development and
Tourism: P.O. Box 800,
111 Syndicate Avenue
South, 2nd Floor
Victoriaville Civic Centre,
Thunder Bay, Ontario,
P7C 5K4 ☎ 807/625-
3960, 800/667-8386 (toll
free)

Old Fort William Historical Park

www.fwhp.ca
✉ Vickers Heights Post
Office, Thunder Bay,
Ontario, P0T 2Z0
☎ 807/473-2344
🕐 Daily, mid-May to mid-
Oct
🍴 Cantine Restaurant ($)
♿ Few
✋ Expensive; moderate in
May and Oct, when
activities are reduced
❓ Trading Post gift store

*Quilting is just one of the
many traditional old crafts
still practised at Upper
Canada Village*

www.uppercanadavillage.com
 69F3
✉ Rural Road 1, Morrisburg,
Ontario, K0C 1X0
☎ 613/543-3704
🕐 Daily, late May–early Oct
🍴 Willard's Hotel ($$),
Harvest Barn Restaurant
($), Village Café ($)
♿ Good ✋ Expensive
❓ Village Store – excellent
Canadiana gift shop

THUNDER BAY ✪✪

Thunder Bay is located deep in the heart of the continent on the northwest shore of Lake Superior, at the head of navigation to the Great Lakes from the Atlantic. As such, it has been an important port and place of exchange at several times in its history. In the early 19th century, furs dominated the local economy, while most recently grain was handled here – huge elevators still dominate the skyline today. Grain markets have changed, however, so that Canada's wheat now makes its way west to Vancouver.

The fur trade era is brilliantly re-created at **Old Fort William**, where you step back to the year 1815 when the canoes of the *voyageurs* filled the lakes and rivers, and a great rendezvous was held here every year to exchange pelts for trade goods. The reconstructed fort is huge, with more than 40 buildings, and is peopled by a whole cast of characters who bring this colorful time to life.

UPPER CANADA VILLAGE ✪✪

This imaginative, fascinating and fun complex, located in a rural setting beside the St. Lawrence River, reproduces early life in what is now Ontario. It is not a museum as such, but a re-creation of a slice of life as it was 150 years ago. At the time, this area of Ontario was settled by Loyalists, who worked hard to establish prosperous farms and small businesses. While strolling round the village, you will meet the inhabitants as they go about their daily tasks: They spin wool, make cheese, grind flour, carve furniture, tend livestock and travel around in all manner of horse-drawn conveyances.

Where To...

Above: *Eaton Centre, Toronto*
Right: *motel sign, Québec*

91

Atlantic Provinces & Québec

Atlantic Provinces

Annapolis Royal, Nova Scotia
Garrison House Dining Room ($$$)
In a 19th-century house opposite Fort Anne. Good food in small intimate dining rooms. Seafood specialties.
⊠ 350 St. George Street
☎ 902/532-5750

Big Pond, Nova Scotia
Rita's ($)
Tearoom run by Canadian singer-songwriter Rita MacNeil in her home town. Specializes in delicious baked goods and fresh tea.
⊠ Big Pond, Cape Breton
☎ 902/828-2667 🅶 Closed mid-Oct to May

Caraquet, New Brunswick
Hotel Paulin Dining Room ($$)
Small hotel dining room serving fresh seafood caught in the Gulf of St. Lawrence, notably scallops and mussels, as well as traditional Acadian fare.
⊠ 143 boulevard St-Pierre Ouest ☎ 506/727-9981

Charlottetown, Prince Edward Island
Gahan House ($$)
Traditional brew-pub with above-average food, including fish and chips coated in batter incorporating the brewery's own ale.
⊠ 126 Sydney Street
☎ 902/626-2337

Fredericton, New Brunswick
Brewbakers ($$)
Seafood, crispy pizza and interesting salads served in a warren of rooms as well as on an outdoor patio and in the bar.
⊠ 546 King Street ☎ 506/459-0067

Halifax, Nova Scotia
McKelvie's Seafood Restaurant ($$$)
In a refurbished firehouse with an outdoor patio in the summer months. A great place for seafood, pasta, chowders, and desserts.
⊠ 1680 Lower Water Street
☎ 902/421-6161

Ryan Duffy's Steak and Seafood ($$)
Great steak cooked to order, plus a wide range of seafood.
⊠ 5640 Spring Garden Road
☎ 902/421-1116

Salty's on the Waterfront ($$)
Waterfront restaurant splendidly located in the Historic Properties area. Excellent lobster, mussels, scallops and salmon.
⊠ 1869 Upper Water Street
☎ 902/423-6818

Mobile, Newfoundland
Captain's Table ($$)
Named after Captain William Jackman, a Newfoundland hero. Great seafood, chowder and other traditional Newfoundland dishes. Pleasant dining room with open fireplace.
⊠ Mobile ☎ 709/334-2278

Moncton, New Brunswick
Maverick's Steak and Lobster House ($$$)
Upscale restaurant specializing in excellent

steak, great chowders and generous desserts.

✉ 40 Weldon Street ☎ 506/855-3346

Saint John, New Brunswick
🍷 🍷 Incredible Edibles Café ($)
Fresh pasta dishes and salads served in a series of small rooms or on an outdoor terrace in summer.

✉ 42 Princess Street
☎ 506/633-7554

🍷 🍷 Mexicali Rosa's ($$)
New Mexican in its atmosphere, with an adobe-style dining room that serves Tex-Mex cuisine with flair.

✉ 88 Prince William Street
☎ 506/652-5252

St. John's, Newfoundland
🍷🍷🍷 Cabot Club ($$$)
In Fairmont Newfoundland Hotel. Specializes in Newfoundland food, excellently prepared and served in a spectacular dining room with views of Signal Hill.

✉ Cavendish Square
☎ 709/726-4980

🍷🍷🍷 The Cellar ($$)
Fine dining with some local dishes and an extensive wine list.

✉ 152 Water Street
☎ 709/579-8900

Souris, Prince Edward Island
The Inn at Bay Fortune ($$)
Splendid views of the Northumberland Strait and a contemporary menu with an emphasis on fresh ingredients.

✉ Route 310 ☎ 902/687-3745
🕐 Closed late Oct to mid-May

Summerside, Prince Edward Island
🍷 Starlite Diner ($$)
A 1950s-style diner, complete with jukeboxes in the booths. Home-style cooking, including fried clams, burgers, barbecued chicken, hot dogs and great desserts.

✉ 810 Water Street ☎ 902/436-7752

Québec

Montréal
🍷 🍷 Alpenhaus ($$)
On the corner with busy rue Ste-Catherine. Swiss restaurant specializing in both cheese and chocolate fondues, veal escalopes, and entrecôte steaks.

✉ 1279 rue St-Marc ☎ 514/935-2285 🚇 Guy-Concordia

🍷 Bar-B Barn ($)
A barn of a place with no frills, but the ribs are great and the chicken's not bad either.

✉ 1201 rue Guy ☎ 514/931-3811
🚇 Guy-Concordia

🍷 Ben's Deli ($)
Montréal institution famous for its smoked-meat sandwiches and cheesecake. The décor hasn't changed since the 1950s.

✉ 990 boulevard de Maisonneuve ☎ 514/844-1000
🚇 Peel

🍷🍷🍷 Bonaparte ($$)
Pretty restaurant in Old Montréal. Fairly classical French cuisine with an emphasis on fresh produce.

✉ 443 rue St-François-Xavier
☎ 514/844-4368 🚇 Place d'Armes

Live Lobsters
Deer Island in Passamaquoddy Bay (► 36) boasts a number of enormous lobster pounds in the various sheltered coves around the island. These function as holding structures where lobsters are kept for shipment to local and international markets. The pounds were first constructed in the late 1920s, and Deer Island is renowned for having the world's largest, at Northern Harbour on the west coast. Together, the pens can store up to 3 million of these sought-after shellfish at any one time.

Famous Products
• The Niagara peninsula is an important wine-producing area. Ice wine is a particular specialty (► 98).
• In spring, the maple trees offer up their sap, which is then boiled down to make maple syrup. Pour the thick taffy on the snow to eat it the traditional way.
• True to the region's French heritage, Québec farmers produce a wide range of delicious cheeses.
• Newfoundland has several highly original food delicacies: Try "figgy duff" for dessert, washed down with a glass of "screech" (potent Jamaican rum).

Second Cup

All over Québec, you will find outlets of Second Cup, Canada's number one specialty coffee retailer. And they have it all – hot coffee, iced coffee, espresso, smooth *caffe latte*, vanilla-bean latte, *chai latte*, the chocolatey decadence of "Chocolate Lover's Latte," maple syrup latte, and "Maple Crème" (steamed milk, maple syrup, and premium white chocolate, topped with whipped cream and a sprinkling of crushed maple sugar).

Bring Your Own Bottle

In Montréal, restaurants with no liquor license allow patrons to *apportez votre vin* (bring your own bottle). They will uncork it for you and provide glasses, but there may be a small corkage charge. They'll even direct you to the nearest *dépanneur* (convenience store) where you can buy your bottle.

Buffet Maharaja ($)

Huge choice of dishes at this Indian buffet, which advertises itself as the largest such restaurant in North America.

✉ 1481 boulevard René-Lévesque Ouest ☎ 514/934-0655 Ⓜ Guy-Concordia, Lucien L'Allier

Café des Beaux-Arts ($$)

In the Montréal Museum of Fine Arts, this restaurant is as elegant as the artworks that surround it. Venison and duck are on the menu, along with deer.

✉ 1384 rue Sherbrooke Ouest ☎ 514/843-3233 Ⓒ Lunch Tue-Sun; dinner Wed Ⓜ Guy-Concordia

Gibby's ($$$)

In fine stone buildings in Old Montréal. First and foremost a steak house, though there is also plenty of fish on the menu.

✉ 298 place d'Youville ☎ 514/282-1837 Ⓒ Closed lunch Ⓜ Place Victoria

House of Jazz/Maison de Jazz ($$)

Formerly Biddles, this club has a long tradition of providing great ribs and the best jazz in the city.

✉ 2060 rue Aylmer ☎ 514/842-8656 Ⓜ McGill, Place-des-Arts

Le Commensal ($)

One of a chain of vegetarian restaurants where you help yourself to a wide choice of dishes and pay by weight.

✉ 1204 avenue McGill College ☎ 514/871-1480 Ⓜ McGill

Le Piment Rouge ($$$)

Sophisticated, elegant restaurant serving excellent, well-presented Szechuan shrimp, chicken, duck and beef dishes.

✉ 1170 rue Peel ☎ 514/866-7816 Ⓜ Peel

L'Express ($$)

Popular, unpretentious bistro with good seafood, bouillabaisse, steak tartare and wonderful *frites* (fries). Reservations essential.

✉ 3927 rue St-Denis ☎ 514/845-5333 Ⓜ Sherbrooke then bus 144

Milos ($$$)

Top-notch Greek restaurant with the freshest fish and vegetables in the city, flown in directly from Greece on occasion.

✉ 5357 avenue du Parc ☎ 514/272-3522) 🚌 Bus 80

Nuances ($$$)

Gourmet French cuisine on the top floor of the casino, with top prices too. Great views over the St. Lawrence River. Business attire.

✉ Casino de Montréal, Parc Jean-Drapeau ☎ 514/392-2708 Ⓜ Jean-Drapeau then free shuttle bus

Soto ($$)

Elegant Japanese restaurant with up to 80 different varieties of sushi and 20 different brands of sake.

✉ 500 rue McGill ☎ 514/864-5115 Ⓜ Square Victoria

Stash Café ($$)

In Old Montréal. Popular bistro-type restaurant serving Polish fare such as pirogies, cabbage rolls, bigos (sauerkraut stew) and borscht.

✉ 200 rue St-Paul Ouest ☎ 514/845-6611 Ⓜ Place d'Armes

🍷🍷 Weinstein and Gavino's Pasta Bar ($$)

Trendy Italian restaurant in the middle of the bar and nightclub district along Crescent Street. Good pizza, pasta, soups, and special salads.

✉ 1434 rue Crescent ☎ 514/288-2231 🚇 Guy-Concordia

Witloof ($$)

Belgian restaurant on trendy street. Great mussels and steak tartare, excellent *frîtes* (fries) and special endive (*witloof* in Flemish) salad.

✉ 3619 rue St-Denis ☎ 514/281-0100 🚇 Sherbrooke

Mont-Tremblant

La Table Enchantée ($$)

Pretty restaurant with attractive gardens. Game, caribou and traditional Québec cuisine.

✉ 1842 Route 117 Nord ☎ 819/425-7113

🍷 Micro Brasserie Le Diable ($)

Really bustles in the evening, especially after a long day of skiing. Excellent beer brewed on the spot.

✉ 1000 chemin des Voyageurs ☎ 819/681-4546

Percé

🍷🍷🍷 Hôtel La Normandie Dining Room ($$$)

Sensational location overlooking Rocher Percé. Seafood and fish dishes with great originality and flair.

✉ 221 Route 132 Ouest ☎ 418/782-2112

Québec City

🍷🍷 Au Petit Coin Breton ($$)

In the Upper Town of Old Québec. Serves nearly 80 varieties of crepes with both savory and sweet fillings.

✉ 1029 rue St-Jean ☎ 418/694-0758

🍷🍷 Aux Anciens Canadiens ($$)

Charming restaurant in a 17th-century house in the Upper Town. Specializes in traditional Québec cuisine – meat pies (*tourtières*) and casseroles.

✉ 34 rue St-Louis ☎ 418/692-1627

🍷🍷🍷 Charles-Baillairge ($$$)

Classy, popular restaurant in the Clarendon Hotel in Upper Town. Refined cuisine and piano chamber music.

✉ 57 rue Ste-Anne ☎ 418/692-2480

🍷🍷 🍷🍷 Guido Le Gourmet ($$$)

Very stylish restaurant in Old Québec (Upper Town). Specializes in French cuisine dishes featuring lobster, quail, veal and salmon.

✉ 73 rue Ste-Anne ☎ 418/692-3856

🍷🍷 🍷🍷 Laurie Raphael ($$)

In the Old Port area of Lower Town. International cuisine with a contemporary flavor. Especially popular at lunchtime; reservations essential.

✉ 117 rue Dalhousie ☎ 418/692-4555

🍷🍷 Le Cochon Dingue ($$)

Café-bistro par excellence in Lower Town. Excellent *frîtes* (fries), mussels and desserts *cochon* (*cochon dingue* means "crazy pig").

✉ 46 boulevard Champlain ☎ 418/692-2013

Montréal Smoked Meat

When Montréalers talk about "smoked meat," they don't mean pastrami or corned beef. Montréal smoked meat is beef massaged with spices, marinated, and then smoked (hence the name). The result is melt-in-your-mouth tender. It is sliced thin, heaped in a pile between two slices of rye bread, and generally served with fries, coleslaw, and a large pickle. You can find smoked-meat sandwiches all over the city, but there are a few institutions famous for them – namely, Schwartz's, Dunn's and Ben's (▶ 93).

Ontario

The Fruits of Niagara

The rich soil and mild climate of the Niagara Peninsula has made it Canada's major fruit-growing and wine-making region. In season, roadside stands sell strawberries, raspberries, cherries, apples, peaches, pears, apricots and grapes. One of the largest outlets is Kurtz Orchards and Country Market (16006 Niagara Parkway), with a magnificent array of fruits and jams (daily, Apr–Dec).

Gananoque

🛆🛆🛆 Gananaque Inn ($–$$)

In the Thousand Islands area. This inn (▶ 102). Formal dining room serving Continental fare; informal pub with a summer patio and light menu (pasta, burgers, etc.).

✉ 550 Stone Street South
☎ 613/382-2165

Kingston

🛆🛆🛆 Chez Piggy ($$)

An interesting downtown restaurant with a garden patio that is very popular with the local literati from Queens University and the Royal Military College.

✉ 68-R Princess Street
☎ 613/549-7673

🛆🛆🛆 The River Mill ($$)

The quintessential Canadian dining room, overlooking the Cataraqui River. Quiet, relaxed, and conservative, and the salmon is very good.

✉ 2 Cataraqui Street
☎ 613/549-5759

Niagara Falls

🛆🛆🛆 Queenston Heights Restaurant ($$)

Relaxed, affordable restaurant overlooking the Niagara River; outdoor patio in summer. Far from the bustle and noise of the falls.

✉ 14184 Niagara Parkway
☎ 905/262-4274 ⊘ Closed Feb–Mar

Niagara-on-the-Lake

🛆🛆 Fan's Court ($$)

On what might be described as the most attractive main street in Eastern Canada. Very good Chinese cuisine inside or on a pretty courtyard in summer.

✉ 135 Queen Street
☎ 905/468-4511

Terroir la Cachette ($$$)

Try a taste of Provence at this upscale restaurant located in the Strewn Winery – fish soup, duck confit, Provençal tart with braised onion and roasted peppers. Choose a wine from the exclusively Ontarian list to accompany it.

✉ 1339 Lakeshore Road
☎ 905/468-1222

Ottawa

🛆🛆 Courtyard Restaurant ($$)

Good Continental cuisine in an old stone building in a courtyard off Sussex Drive near the Byward Market.

✉ 21 George Street
☎ 613/241-1516

🛆🛆 Fish Market Restaurant ($$)

Busy restaurant in Byward Market serving fresh fish and seafood from all over the world. TExtensive wine list.

✉ 54 York Street ☎ 613/241-3474

Johnny Farina ($$)

Good Italian food in the setting of the old Elgin movie theater. Innovative pasta dishes, pizzas from the wood-oven and sumptuous home-made desserts and biscotti.

✉ 216 Elgin Street ☎ 613/565-5155

🛆🛆🛆 Le Café ($$)

In the National Arts Centre overlooking the Rideau Canal, with seating on a pleasant outdoor terrace beside the canal in summer. Gourmet restaurant offering well-prepared Canadian specialties.

✉ 53 Elgin Street ☎ 613/594-5127 ⊘ Closed Sun

▼▼▼ Merlot ($$$)
Revolving restaurant in the Marriott Hotel, with splendid views of the city and its site on the Ottawa River. Expensive, varied menu.
🖂 100 Kent Street ☎ 613/783-4212

Sault Ste. Marie
▼▼▼ A Thymely Manner ($$)
In an old home. Uses only the best ingredients, herbs and spices for its menu of steak, pasta, and fish.
🖂 531 Albert Street East ☎ 705/759-3262

Sudbury
▼▼ Culpepper's Eatery ($)
Enormous choice of Italian and Greek specialties, as well as traditional burgers, wings and a salad bar.
🖂 1853 Regent Street South ☎ 705/522-2422

Thunder Bay
▼▼▼ White Fox Inn Dining Room ($$)
First-class dining combining Canadian and European influences at a small inn just south of the city overlooking the Nor'Wester Mountains (► 103).
🖂 1345 Mountain Road ☎ 807/577-3699

Toronto
Auberge du Pommier ($$$)
Charming North End restaurant located in a "cottage-style" home. Excellent contemporary French cuisine.
🖂 4150 Yonge Street ☎ 416/222-2220 🚇 York Mills ⓒ Closed Sun

▼▼▼ Bistro 990 ($$$)
French bistro straight out of Paris. Serves excellent shrimp and filet mignon.
🖂 990 Bay Street ☎ 416/921-9990 🚇 Wellesley ⓒ Closed Sat lunch and Sun

Boujadi ($$$)
Authentic Moroccan cuisine cooked to perfection with just the right amount of spice. Choose from tasty couscous, home-made *merguez* beef sausages and traditional tagines. You may have to wait for a table but it will be worth it.
🖂 2999 Eglinton Avenue West ☎ 416/440-0258 🚇 Eglinton West

Centro Grill and Wine Bar ($$$)
Popular with visiting celebrities. Contemporary cuisine highlighting Canadian ingredients such as lamb and venison.
🖂 2472 Yonge Street ☎ 416/483-2211 🚇 Eglinton ⓒ Closed Sun

▼▼▼ Courtyard Café ($$$)
In the Windsor Arms Hotel near the University of Toronto campus. Luxurious restaurant with excellent rack of lamb and salmon, as well as afternoon tea served in a relaxed atmosphere.
🖂 18 St. Thomas Street ☎ 416/971-9666 🚇 Bay ⓒ Closed Sun–Mon

▼▼▼ Jacques Bistro ($$)
Small, intimate spot in the heart of Yorkville serving French cuisine. Lunch is very good value. There's excellent salmon, seafood, veal, lamb and wonderful desserts.
🖂 126A Cumberland Street (2nd floor) ☎ 416/961-1893 🚇 Bay

Ice Wine
Southern Ontario has a flourishing wine industry with more than 60 wineries. At latitude 43°N, the Niagara peninsula is in fact south of most of Burgundy, France, and at the same latitude as northern California. The most famous product of the area is ice wine, which is made from grapes that have been frozen solid on the vine. The resulting yellow liquid is rich, luscious and highly prized by connoisseurs. This expensive tipple is known as Ontario's "yellow gold."

Peameal Bacon on a Bun

While visiting Toronto, you might want to try this local favorite. Peameal bacon is salt- and sugar-cured extra-lean ham, rolled in cornmeal. Torontonians eat it for breakfast cooked and hot on a bun. You will find it on restaurant menus, or go to the St. Lawrence Market (► 106), where the peameal bacon sandwiches are famous.

♦♦♦♦ North 44 ($$$)

Sophisticated restaurant with creative Continental cuisine and impeccable service. Duck is a specialty. Large wine list, also by the glass.
✉ 2537 Yonge Street
☎ 416/487-4897 🚇 Eglinton

♦♦♦ Opus on Prince Arthur ($$$)

In a converted brownstone house close to Yorkville. Excellent Californian cuisine and an extensive wine list to choose from.
✉ 37 Prince Arthur Avenue
☎ 416/921-3105 🚇 St. George

♦♦ Pan on the Danforth ($$)

Upscale Greek dining with a rather eclectic menu, which has been described as "nouveau Greek." Good moussaka and a delicious casserole of chopped beef and potato.
✉ 516 Danforth Avenue
☎ 416/466-8158 🚇 Closed lunch 🚇 Pape, Chester

♦♦♦ Panagaea ($$)

Stylish restaurant serving fresh market cuisine at lunch and dinner, notably shellfish and sirloin steak. Also afternoon tea for tired shoppers.
✉ 1221 Bay Street ☎ 416/920-2323 🚇 Bay 🚇 Closed Sun

♦♦ Pier 4 Storehouse Restaurant ($$)

Two-story warehouse on the waterfront with a marine décor. Focuses on fresh seafood – the lobster, crab, and shrimp are particularly good.
✉ 245 Queens Quay West
☎ 416/203-1440 🚇 Union then Harbourfront streetcar 509 or 510 🚇 Closed Mon

Real Thailand ($$)

Superb Thai food – start with the shrimp appetizers, soup or satay then move on to one of the many main courses. Dessert is limited to just three choices.
✉ 350 Bloor Street West
☎ 416/924-7444 🚇 Spadina

♦♦♦ Scaramouche ($$$)

Just north of downtown. Romantic candlelit luxury, with splendid views of the Toronto skyline and acclaimed cuisine.
✉ 1 Benvenuto Place
☎ 416/961-8011 🚇 Closed lunch and Sun 🚇 Summerhill

♦♦ Shopsy's Deli and Restaurant ($)

Shopsy's is a popular and noisy place close to the financial district with a huge menu of sandwiches, subs, soups and salads. One of several outlets – also on King Street and 1535 Yonge Street.
✉ 33 Yonge Street ☎ 416/365-3333 🚇 Union, King

Tiger Lily's Noodle House ($–$$)

Very popular lunch stop with just about everyone. Noodles feature prominently but there is also great dim sum, *pad Thai* and spring rolls to choose from.
✉ 257 Queen Street West
☎ 416/977-5499 🚇 Osgoode

♦♦♦♦ Truffles ($$$)

In the Four Seasons Hotel. A very swanky place, with prices to match, and generally considered to be the best restaurant in town. Contemporary French menu in classy surroundings.
✉ 21 Avenue Road ☎ 416/964-0411 🚇 Museum, Bay

Atlantic Provinces

Charlottetown, Prince Edward Island

♦♦♦♦ Inns on Great George ($$–$$$)

This inn has several properties, providing luxury accommodations in 19th-century style. Some rooms have fireplace and Jacuzzi, and all are elegantly furnished with antiques. Breakfast included.

✉ 58 Great George Street
☎ 902/892-0606

Dingwall, Nova Scotia

♦♦ Markland Coastal Resort ($$)

At the northern tip of Cape Breton Island. Fabulous site surrounded by mountains and beaches; a series of simple wooden cabins and a good seafood restaurant.

✉ Cabot Trail ☎ 902/383-2246

Fredericton, New Brunswick

♦♦ Lord Beaverbrook Hotel ($$$)

Elegant hotel with unbeatable location downtown near the Legislative Assembly and Beaverbrook Art Gallery (► 35). The Terrace restaurant overlooks the St. John River.

✉ 659 Queen Street ☎ 506/455-3371

Halifax, Nova Scotia

♦♦♦♦ Halliburton House Inn ($$)

Elegantly restored historic property in the old part of town. Rooms are furnished with antiques. Pleasant dining room with a courtyard for light meals in summer. Continental breakfast included.

✉ 5184 Morris Street
☎ 902/420-0658

L'Anse au Clair, Newfoundland

♦♦ Northern Lights Inn ($–$$)

On the Labrador Strait, close to the ferry terminal at St. Barbe; excellent place from which to start a visit to Labrador. Also housekeeping cottages with power hookups; good restaurant.

✉ 58 Main Street ☎ 709/931-2332

Moncton, New Brunswick

♦♦ Chateau Moncton ($$)

Modern hotel perfectly situated for viewing the tidal bore as it races up the Petitcodiac River from the Bay of Fundy. Continental breakfast included.

✉ 100 Main Street ☎ 506/870-4444

North Rustico, Prince Edward Island

♦♦ Gulf View Cottages ($$)

Fully equipped two-bedroom cottages with a fine site overlooking the Gulf of St. Lawrence in Prince Edward Island National Park. Cycling and jogging trails; beach.

✉ Gulf Shore Road ☎ 902/963-2052 🄲 Closed mid-Oct to mid-May

St. John's, Newfoundland

♦♦♦ Murray Premises Hotel ($$$)

Former warehouse overlooking the harbor, restored as a luxurious boutique hotel. Old beams and exposed brickwork beautifully set off the up-to-the-minute facilities. Two restaurants.

✉ 5 Becks Cove
☎ 709/738-7773

Prices

You may expect to pay the following prices per room per night:
$ = under Can$75
$$ = Can$75–150
$$$ = more than Can$150

Opening times

Establishments are open year-round unless indicated otherwise.

Diamond Ratings

AAA field inspectors evaluate and rate lodging establishments based on the overall quality and services. AAA's diamond rating criteria reflect the design and service standards set by the lodging industry, combined with the expectations of members.

Properties rated with one (♦) or two (♦♦) diamonds are clean and well-maintained, offering comfortable rooms, with the two diamond property showing enhancements in décor and furnishings. A three (♦♦♦) diamond property shows marked upgrades in physical attributes, services and comfort and may offer additional amenities. A four (♦♦♦♦) diamond rating signifies a property offering a high level of service and hospitality and a wide variety of amenities and upscale facilities. A five (♦♦♦♦♦) diamond rating represents a world-class facility, offering the highest level of luxurious accommodations and personalized guest services.

Québec

Pierre du Calvet
Pierre du Calvet settled in Montréal at the end of the French regime. As a French-speaking Protestant, he was made a justice of the peace when the British conquered the city in 1760. Fifteen years later, he offered his services to the Americans when they occupied the city, a factor not appreciated by the British, who threw him into prison on their return. Eventually released, he made his way to London to appeal against this injustice but was drowned at sea en route.

Ayer's Cliff
👑👑 👑👑 Auberge Ripplecove Inn ($$$)
In lovely gardens overlooking Lake Massawippi in the Eastern Townships. Attractive hotel with a finely furnished interior, excellent restaurant, summer terrace and outdoor pool.
✉ 700 Ripplecove Road
☎ 819/838-4296

Baie-St-Paul
👑👑👑 Auberge La Maison Otis ($$–$$$)
Delightful hotel with traditional Québec architecture, attractive bedrooms and modern facilities. Pleasant gardens with a summer terrace, swimming pool, and health and beauty suite. Price includes dinner and breakfast
✉ 23 rue St-Jean-Baptiste
☎ 418/435-2255

Montréal
👑👑👑 Auberge de la Fontaine ($$)
Pleasant small hotel in a renovated Victorian house on Lafontaine Park in Montréal's east end. Quiet yet close to vibrant rue Saint-Denis, and with beautifully decorated rooms. Generous Continental breakfast, and guests also have access to the kitchen to prepare their own meals or snacks.
✉ 1301 rue Rachel ☎ 514/597-0166 🚇 Mont-Royal

Auberge du Vieux-Port ($$)
In a refurbished late-19th-century building in Old Montréal with stone walls and wooden beams. Some rooms have views of the St. Lawrence. Excellent restaurant, with rooftop terrace open in summer.
✉ 97 rue de la Commune Est
☎ 514/876-0081 🚇 Place d'Armes

👑👑👑 Château Versailles ($$)
Luxury hotel in a couple of beautifully renovated former town houses with a modern extension across the street. Nice bedrooms with custom-made furniture, plus stylish bar and good restaurant.
✉ 1659 rue Sherbrooke Ouest
☎ 514/933-8111 🚇 Guy-Concordia

👑👑 👑👑 Fairmont Queen Elizabeth ($$–$$$)
Grand dame of downtown accommodations, opened in 1958. Archetypal railroad hotel, built over the train station and connected to the maze of Montréal's Underground City. John Lennon and Yoko Ono held their famous bed-in here and Lennon wrote "Give Peace a Chance." Indoor pool and health club, home of the Beaver Club Restaurant.
✉ 900 boulevard René-Lévesque ☎ 514/861-3511
🚇 Bonaventure, Peel, McGill

Pierre du Calvet ($$$)
Romantic small hotel in Old Montréal, partially located in a French Regime house of 1725 and named for its most famous resident (▶ side panel). The public rooms are full of antiques and family heirlooms; the bedrooms have four-poster beds. Breakfast is served in a sunny Victorian conservatory. Restaurant on the premises.
✉ 405 rue Bonsecours
☎ 514/282-1725 🚇 Champ-de-Mars

Mont-Tremblant

♥♥♥ ♥♥♥ Fairmont Tremblant ($$–$$$)

Part of the enormous Tremblant resort complex, and splendidly located with views of mountain and village. Rooms are fairly standard – except for the views. Swimming pools and health club on site.

✉ 3045 chemin de la Chapelle
☎ 819/681-7000

Percé

♥♥♥ Le Mirage ($–$$)

Family-run hotel where every room has large windows and fabulous views of Percé's famous rock. Pleasant dining room, extensive grounds, tennis court and outdoor pool. Whale-watching boat trips can be arranged.

✉ 288 Route 132 Ouest
☎ 418/782-5151 ◎ Closed mid-Oct to mid-May

Québec City

♥♥♥ Auberge St-Antoine ($$$)

In a once derelict warehouse in the Lower Town, this hotel has great originality and flair. Some of the rooms are whimsical – there's a 007 suite, for example – and some have a rooftop terrace.

✉ 10 rue St-Antoine
☎ 418/692-2211

♥♥♥ ♥♥♥ Fairmont Le Château Frontenac ($$–$$$)

Dominates the Upper Town with its towers and turrets, one of the few in the world that is so much a part of the image of its city. Rooms are pleasant; those with any kind of view are sought after and expensive. Large swimming pool and spa; variety of restaurants.

✉ 1 rue des Carrières
☎ 418/692-3861

♥♥♥ Le Priori ($$)

In an 18th-century building in the Lower Town. Stylish hotel with old-fashioned bedrooms and some loft-style suites with kitchens. Continental breakfast included; restaurant with terrace on site.

✉ 15 rue Sault-au-Matelot
☎ 418/692-3992

♥♥♥ L'Hôtel du Capitole ($$)

Part of the complex that includes the Capitole Theatre. Just outside the walls of the Upper Town but within easy walking distance of everything. Rooms are modern and interestingly decorated with decidedly theatrical themes.

✉ 972 rue St-Jean ☎ 418/694-4040

♥♥ L'Hôtel du Vieux-Québec ($$)

Pleasant hotel with an eccentric system of staircases leading to no-frills rooms with exposed stone walls. Continental breakfast included; bistro and terrace in summer. Minimum two-night stay.

✉ 1190 rue Saint-Jean
☎ 418/692-1850

Wakefield

Wakefield Mill ($$)

Lovely inn in a 19th-century water mill on the La Pêche River north of Ottawa. Some rooms have exposed brick walls and hardwood floors, and some have views of the adjacent falls. Suites are housed in a converted grain silo. Breakfast included.

✉ 60 Mill Road ☎ 819/459-1838

Camping

For an inexpensive vacation, you could consider camping. Eastern Canada has wonderful campgrounds in both its national and provincial parks, as well as full-service private sites. Campsites also often give you access to lakes or rivers for water-oriented activities such as boating, canoeing, and swimming.

► 120 for addresses of tourist information offices, which can supply lists of campgrounds.

Ontario

Bed-and-breakfasts
Another inexpensive option is the ever-increasing number of bed-and-breakfast establishments. Any local tourist office can supply a list and will often help you make reservations. The major cities – Toronto, Montréal, Québec and Ottawa – all have fairly extensive networks. And, of course, breakfast is included.

Gananoque
☗☗☗ **Gananoque Inn ($$)**
Beside the St. Lawrence in the Thousand Islands area. Historic inn with spectacular views of the Thousand Islands. Rooms are located in several different buildings, some of them on the waterfront. Dining room with exceptionally good food (► 96). Boat rentals, fishing.
✉ **550 Stone Street South**
☎ **613/382-2165**

Hamilton
☗☗☗ **Visitors Inn ($$)**
Above-average hotels in the city center. Rooms are stylish and some have kitchenettes. Indoor pool, fitness center; dining room.
✉ **649 Main Street West**
☎ **905/529-6979**

Kingston
☗☗ **Peachtree Inn ($$)**
Excellent location with easy access to the city, highways and shopping. Spacious rooms and loft-style suites.
✉ **1187 Princess Street**
☎ **613/546-4411**

Niagara Falls
☗☗ ☗☗ **Sheraton Fallsview ($$$)**
The best place in Niagara Falls – it is a high-rise structure with fabulous views of both the Canadian and American falls. Indoor pool, dining room (with views) and very high prices.
✉ **6755 Fallsview Boulevard**
☎ **905/374-1077**

Niagara-on-the-Lake
☗☗ ☗☗ **Pillar and Post Inn ($$$)**
Lovely old inn (1890) in the heart of charming Niagara-on-the-Lake. Rooms are pleasantly Victorian in atmosphere. Full spa; excellent dining room.
✉ **48 John Street** ☎ **905/468-2123**

Nobel
☗☗ ☗☗ **Winnetou Resort ($$–$$$)**
On the shores of Georgian Bay, with sandy beach and rocky shore. Rustic fully equipped cottages; outdoor barbecue and deck furniture. Health center; boating and fishing possibilities.
✉ **Dillon Road, Rural Route 1**
☎ **705/342-9967**

Ottawa
☗☗☗ **Arc, The Hotel ($$–$$$)**
Stylish boutique hotel centrally located close to the Parliament Buildings. Chic and popular, with elegant, well-equipped rooms.
✉ **140 Slater Street** ☎ **613/238-2888**

☗☗ ☗☗ **Fairmont Château Laurier ($$$)**
A magnificent château-style hotel in the heart of the capital. It is famous for the fact that the original table linen and silverware went down with the *Titanic*! Swimming pool, fitness center, restaurant and attractive outdoor terrace.
✉ **1 Rideau Street** ☎ **613/241-1414**

☗☗☗ **Lord Elgin Hotel ($$)**
A city landmark just across the street from the National Arts Centre. For what it offers (rather small but well-appointed rooms), it is remarkably good value. Restaurant on premises.
✉ **100 Elgin Street** ☎ **613/235-3333**

Sault Ste. Marie

▼▼▼ Algoma Water Tower Inn ($$)

Motor inn on the north side of town with excellent facilities. Some rooms have wood-burning stoves and pine furniture. Good place for children, with a swimming pool and fitness center, landscaped courtyard and Lone Star Restaurant.

✉ 360 Great Northern Road
☎ 705/949-8111

Thunder Bay

▼▼▼ White Fox Inn ($$–$$$)

In a large wooded estate just south of the city with nice views of the surrounding hills. Small but delightful inn offering pleasant, well-furnished rooms and the best food in the area (➤ 97).

✉ 1345 Mountain Road
☎ 807/577-3699

Toronto

▼▼▼ Cambridge Suites Hotel ($$$)

Classy hotel in the middle of the financial district and close to theaters. Two-room suites with microwave and refrigerator. On the upper floors, suites have splendid city views. Continental breakfast included.

✉ 15 Richmond Street East
☎ 416/368-1990 🚇 Queen

▼▼ ▼▼ Fairmont Royal York ($$–$$$)

Long a Toronto landmark and institution. Huge hotel (nearly 1,400 rooms) connected to the train station and the underground PATH system. Amazing lobby with chandeliers and handpainted ceiling. Elegant rooms and a pleasant indoor skylit pool and fitness center.

✉ 100 Front Street West,
☎ 416/368-2511 🚇 Union

▼▼▼ Renaissance Toronto at SkyDome ($$$)

The only hotel on the continent directly connected to a sports stadium – 70 of its rooms overlook the SkyDome (➤ panel). Room rates vary depending on what's going on in the city.

✉ 1 Blue Jays Way ☎ 416/341-7100 🚇 Union then Skywalk

▼▼ ▼▼ Sheraton Centre ($$)

Huge but reasonably priced hotel in a central location opposite City Hall, linked to the PATH underground network and close to theaters. Spacious, well appointed rooms. Fitness spa and indoor/outdoor pool.

✉ 123 Queen Street East
☎ 416/361-1000 🚇 Queen, Osgoode

▼▼ ▼▼ Westin Harbour Castle ($$$)

Superb location on the waterfront. Large but classy hotel with first-rate rooms. Revolving restaurant on the rooftop with great views of the harbor and city; indoor pool and fitness center.

✉ 1 Harbour Square ☎ 416/869-1600 🚇 Union

▼▼ ▼▼ Windsor Arms ($$$)

On a quiet street just south of busy Bloor Street, close to Yorkville and the University of Toronto campus. Luxury five-story hotel with tastefully furnished rooms, all with whirlpool baths. Excellent restaurant, the Courtyard Café (➤ 97).

✉ 18 St. Thomas Street
☎ 416/971-9666 🚇 Bay

Room with a View

When staying at the Renaissance Toronto at SkyDome, take care if your room overlooks the stadium. Television camera crews covering games here adore showing the viewers anything going on in the rooms – especially if it has nothing to do with the action on the field!

Shopping Centers & Complexes

Opening Times
The shopping centers and complexes listed open daily, year-round, unless otherwise noted.

Shopping Centers
With a few notable exceptions, shopping centers tend to be located on the edges of cities where land is available for plentiful parking. Throughout Eastern Canada, these malls are where you will find food supermarkets. Shopping centers are generally open seven days a week, although on Sundays hours may be reduced and some stores will open only at midday.

Atlantic Provinces

Fredericton, New Brunswick
Regent Mall
South of the city near the Trans-Canada Highway. Bright, airy mall with 115 stores, including a range of boutiques, Sears, Wal-Mart and Chapters. Food court.
✉ 1381 Regent Street
☎ 506/452-1005

Halifax, Nova Scotia
Halifax Shopping Centre
To the west of downtown. Biggest mall in Halifax, with over 150 stores, including boutiques, sports stores, pharmacies, banks, Sears and Wal-Mart. Fast-food outlets.
✉ 7001 Mumford Road
☎ 902/453-1752

Moncton, New Brunswick
Champlain Place
In the suburb of Dieppe, southeast of the city. Largest mall in Atlantic Canada, with specialty stores, fashion, sports and electronics stores, Sears, Sobeys supermarket and Wal-Mart. Movie theater complex and amusement park; food court with restaurants.
✉ 477 Paul Street ☎ 506/857-0040

St. John's, Newfoundland
Avalon Mall
Northwest of the city. Attractive mall on two levels, with clothing, books, music, gifts and jewelry stores, Sobeys supermarket and Wal-Mart. Large movie theater complex; food court and restaurants.
✉ 48 Kenmount Road
☎ 709/753-7144

Québec

Montréal
Complexe Desjardins
On east side of downtown linked to the Underground City. Has a vast central atrium complete with fountain and exhibitions. Fashion stores, liquor store, IGA supermarket, pharmacy, Dollarama and gift stores. Food court and restaurants.
✉ 150 rue Ste-Catherine Ouest or 175 boulevard René-Lévesque Ouest ☎ 514/281-1870 Ⓜ Place-des-Arts

Marché Bonsecours
In Old Montréal. The building originally served as city hall and covered farmers' market. Today, it houses an excellent collection of boutiques selling crafts, fashion, jewelry, home wares and furniture. Several restaurants.
✉ 350 rue St-Paul Est ☎ 514/872-7730 Ⓜ Champ-de-Mars

Montréal Eaton Centre
Large shopping complex linked into the Underground City, with about 150 fashion stores, banks and other retail outlets. Best known for being open until 9 pm every weekday (the rest of downtown closes up at 6 pm Mon–Wed). Food court.
✉ 705 rue Ste-Catherine Ouest
☎ 514/288-3708 Ⓜ McGill

Québec City
Place Fleur-de-Lys
West of the city. Stylish mall with around 250 stores. In addition to the clothing boutiques, you will find Sears, The Bay and Mega Sports. Fast food and restaurants.
✉ 550 boulevard Wilfrid-Hamel
☎ 418/529-0728 Ⓜ Closed Sun

Place Laurier
West of downtown. Largest mall in Québec, with 350 stores, including Zellers, The Bay, Sears, leisure boutiques, and clothing, sports and home wares stores. Fast food and restaurants.
✉ 2700 boulevard Laurier
☎ 418/651-7085

Ste-Anne-de-Beaupré
Promenades Ste-Anne
Close to the Ste-Anne-de-Beaupré shrine (► 57). Discount strip mall where you can find substantial savings on designer labels in sportswear, leisurewear, footwear, fashion accessories and home wares. Restaurant on site.
✉ 10909 boulevard Ste-Anne
☎ 418/827-3555

Sherbrooke
Carrefour de l'Estrie
Just west of the city. Largest mall in the Eastern Townships, with about 200 stores and 20 restaurants. Sears, The Bay, Zellers and Simons are here, along with a range of other stores. Food court with great choice of eateries.
✉ 3050 boulevard de Portland
☎ 819/563-1907

Ontario

Kingston
Cataraqui Town Centre
Near the Trans-Canada Highway just west of the Cataraqui River. Has more than 140 stores, including The Bay, Zellers and Sears, plus a range of smaller ones. Children's area; fast food and restaurants.
✉ 945 Gardiners Road
☎ 613/389-7900

Niagara Falls
Canada One Factory Outlets
About 40 stores selling designer items with huge discounts, among them Liz Claiborne, Danier Leather, Tommy Hilfiger, Ralph Lauren, Levi's, Reebok, Roots, Villeray and Bosch.
✉ 7500 Lundy's Lane
☎ 905/356-8989

Ottawa
Rideau Centre
Right in the heart of the capital. About 200 stores, including innumerable fashion boutiques, specialty stores and Sears. Wide variety of food outlets, including Italian, Mexican and Chinese.
✉ 50 Rideau Street ☎ 613/236-6565

Toronto
Eaton Centre
In the heart of the city. Architecturally stunning shopping center worth the visit even if you don't shop. Eaton's doesn't exist as a department store any more, but there's a Sears and nearly 300 other stores. Wide variety of food outlets and restaurants.
✉ 220 Yonge Street ☎ 416/598-8700 Ⓠ Queen, Dundas

Honest Ed's
An enormous – and somewhat brash – discount retailer and Toronto institution, Honest Ed's has flashing lights outside and acres of bargains inside on all items, especially clothing, food, home wares and gifts.
✉ 581 Bloor Street ☎ 416/537-1574 Ⓠ Bathurst

Queens Quay Terminal
Right on the waterfront. Light, airy former warehouse built in 1926, home to about 50 upscale stores with a Canadian focus. Variety of restaurants and cafés with lake views, and outdoor patios in the summer months.
✉ 207 Queens Quay West
☎ 416/203-0510 Ⓠ Union then Harbourfront streetcar 509 or 510

Farmers' Markets
Right across Eastern Canada, farmers' markets are held in the summer months, usually on Saturday mornings. Check with the local tourist office in any given community to find out when they are on (► 106 for listings of the most well known). Fresh local produce is generally available, as are local crafts. Often they also act as flea markets, selling secondhand books, jewelry and a range of other domestic items.

Public Markets

Opening Times
The markets listed are in operation daily, year-round, unless otherwise noted.

Kitchener Farmers' Market
Kitchener, Ontario, lies in the middle of an area of Mennonite religious farming communities. The Mennonites come to the town's Frederick Street market in their traditional dress by horse and buggy, and sell homebaked breads and pastries, meats of all kinds and specialties such as schnitzel, pigtails, and *koch käse* (cheese). The market is held year-round on Saturday mornings, and on Wednesday mornings Jun–Sep.

Atlantic Provinces

Fredericton, New Brunswick
Boyce Farmers' Market
About 200 vendors offer local produce, crafts and gifts at this longtime institution in downtown.
✉ 665 George Street
☎ 506/451-1815
🕐 Sat 6 am–1 pm

Halifax, Nova Scotia
Halifax Farmers' Market
In the courtyards of a former brewery, this market is a hive of activity on Saturdays.
✉ 1498 Lower Water Street (Brewery Market) ☎ 902/492-4043 🕐 Sat am

Saint John, New Brunswick
City Market
In existence since 1876, this covered market is great for picnic ingredients. Lobsters, cheeses, all kinds of fresh produce and dulse (► 36).
✉ 47 Charlotte Street
☎ 506/658-2820 🕐 Mon–Sat

Québec

Montréal
Atwater Market
Popular market selling local produce, cheese, meat, fish and bread. Acres of flowers in the spring; fruit and vegetables all summer; maple products and a range of alcoholic beverages year-round. Café.
✉ 138 avenue Atwater
☎ 514/937-7754 🚇 Lionel-Groulx

Jean-Talon Market
In the heart of Little Italy, north of the city center. Popular market for fresh fruit and vegetables, with a bakery at its hub. Fish and meat stores and a great cheese store. Café.
✉ 7075 avenue Casgrain
☎ 514/277-1588 🚇 Jean-Talon

Maisonneuve Market
Small market in the east end of the city, with bread, fruit and vegetables. In summer, cultural activities are held in the market square.
✉ 4445 rue Montréal Est
☎ 514/937-7754 🚇 Frontenac then bus 125 east

Québec City
Québec Public Market
In the Old Port. Sells great cheese and bread, wonderful fruit in season, maple products and flowers.
✉ 160 quai St-André
☎ 418/692-2517

Ontario

Ottawa
Byward Market
Historic market in central Ottawa centered around a building selling fine crafts and gifts. Outside, there are stands of fruit and vegetables, and stores selling cheese, meat, bread and wine. Restaurants.
✉ 55 Byward Market Square

Toronto
Kensington Market
► 77

St. Lawrence Market
Offers a wonderful assortment of fresh fruit and vegetables, meat and deli produce, fish, and cheese and dairy foods. Food outlets, pub and peameal bacon sandwiches (► 98).
✉ 92 Front Street East
☎ 416/392-7219 🕐 Closed Sun–Mon 🚇 Union

Crafts, Antiques, & Other Specialties

Atlantic Provinces

Fredericton, New Brunswick

Botanicals Gift Store and Studio
In downtown's historic district. Pretty store in a clapboard house with trailing garden foliage, offering unique pieces by Atlantic provinces craftspeople, including superb floral arrangements by John L. Welling.
✉ **65 Shore Street** ☎ **506/454-7361**

River Valley Crafts and Artisan Gift Shops
A number of craftspeople sell their wares such as painting, jewelry, First Nations crafts and Celtic art on the main floor of the former Soldiers' Barracks in downtown's historic Garrison district.
✉ **Soldiers' Barracks, Carleton Street** ☎ **506/460-2837** ⏲ **Closed Oct–May**

Québec

Granby

Laflamme Fourrures
Eastern Townships family business with all you need to survive the Canadian winter in the way of warm clothing, fur and leather coats by Québec designers.
✉ **328 rue Principale** ☎ **450/378-8484** ⏲ **Closed Sun**

Kahnawake

5 Nations Indian Art Gallery
On the Mohawk reserve just southwest of Montréal. Gallery in a splendid wood building, devoted to Iroquois art and crafts. Forms part of a complex where you can visit longhouses and watch traditional dancing displays.
✉ **Route 138 Est** ☎ **450/638-7777**

Montréal

Bidz
Enormous selection of beads from all over the world, which you can string yourself, plus some unusual pieces made by local artists.
✉ **3945A rue St-Denis** ☎ **514/286-2421** Ⓜ **Mont-Royal**

Dubarry Furs
Downtown furrier with excellent quality: price ratio. Designer and made-to-measure fur coats and a range of accessories.
✉ **370 rue Sherbrooke Ouest** ☎ **514/844-7483** Ⓜ **McGill**

Hemsleys
Jeweller in business since 1870. Unique pieces by local craftspeople, plus crystal, porcelain and sculpture.
✉ **660 rue Ste-Catherine Ouest** ☎ **514/866-3706** Ⓜ **McGill**

Henri Henri
The hat store to beat all hat stores. Great fur hats and classic headgear for men by names such as Biltmore, Borsalino and Stetson.
✉ **189 rue Ste-Catherine Est** ☎ **514/288-0109** ⏲ **Closed Sun** Ⓜ **St-Laurent, Berri-UQAM**

Maison Simons
Highly popular fashion store for men and women, specializing in stylish outfits at moderate prices.
✉ **977 rue Ste-Catherine Ouest** ☎ **514/282-1840** Ⓜ **Peel, McGill**

Ogilvy
In business since 1866. Home to 20 or more fashion franchises, including Aquascutum, Anne Klein and

Opening times
The shops listed are open daily, year-round, unless otherwise noted

Montréal's Antiques District
Rue Notre-Dame Ouest between avenue Atwater and rue Guy has about 30 different antiques stores. Some sell "real" antiques, others are only used-furniture stores, but all are interesting. Most of the stores are concentrated either close to rue Guy or to avenue Atwater – there's a section in the middle with nothing at all. To get there, walk east on Notre-Dame from the Lionel-Groulx métro station; alternatively, take bus 35 south from the Guy-Concordia station, get off at rue Notre-Dame and then walk west.

Canadiana in Ottawa's Museum

The national museums in Ottawa have excellent gift stores offering a variety of Canadian arts and crafts, as well as books and toys. The National Gallery of Canada has an art-oriented store, while Gatineau's Museum of Civilization favors Canadian crafts. The Canada Science and Technology Museum, Canada Aviation Museum and Canadian War Museum are similarly endowed with interesting gift stores.

Guy Laroche. Famous for its bagpiper, who parades through the store at noon.
⊠ 1307 rue Ste-Catherine Ouest ☎ 514/842-7711 ⓖ Peel

Percé
Boutique Au Bon Secours
An artisan-owned craft store in a former pharmacy selling original work by local artists, notably sandstone bird sculptures.
⊠ 150 Route 138 Ouest
☎ 418/782-2011 ⓒ Closed Nov–Apr

Piedmont
Antiquités Hier pour Demain
Québec pine furniture, woodcarvings, folk art and old toys.
⊠ 914 boulevard des Laurentides ☎ 450/227-4231
ⓒ Closed Mon–Thu

Québec City
Artisans du Bas-Canada
Family-run store in the old city. Sells the works of 50 or more Canadian artists and craftspeople, including Inuit and First Nations art.
⊠ 30 côte de la Fabrique
☎ 418/692-2109

Boutique Canadeau
Store in Upper Town selling a range of Canadian-made products, including fur and leather items, jewelry, sweaters and sculptures from Nunavut.
⊠ 1124 rue St-Jean ☎ 418/692-4850

Cuir La Pomme
Stocks the creations of more than a dozen Québec leather designers. You can order custom-made clothes too.
⊠ 47 rue Sous-le-Fort
☎ 418/692-2875

Fourrures du Vieux-Port
Great collection of fur coats, jackets and hats, plus fur-trimmed leather garments – but don't expect things to be cheap.
⊠ 55 rue St-Pierre ☎ 418/692-6686

Galeries d'Art Inuit Brousseau et Brousseau
Next door to the Château Frontenac. Store and gallery devoted to the works of Canada's Inuit artists and sculptors; stocks some superb pieces.
⊠ 35 rue St-Louis ☎ 418/694-1828

Louis Perrier, Joaillier
In the heart of the Lower Town. Exquisite gold jewelry set with a variety of colored stones.
⊠ 48 rue du Petit-Champlain
☎ 418/692-4633

Ontario

Acton
Olde Hide House
The leather store to beat all leather stores. Coats, jackets, pants (trousers), vests, belts, gloves, purses and wallets, in all shapes, sizes and colors.
⊠ 49 Eastern Avenue
☎ 519/853-1031

Elora
Karger Gallery
Sells the works of 100 or more Canadian craftspeople, in ceramics, glass, wood, metal and on canvas.
⊠ Elora Mews, 45 Mill Street West ☎ 519/846-2921

Niagara-on-the-Lake
Europa Antiques
Wonderful antiques store in an ivy-covered church building just outside Niagara-

on-the-Lake. Furniture and a range of small items.

✉ 1523 Niagara Stone Road (Highway 55) ☎ 905/468-3130 ◉ Closed Mon and Tue except by appointment

French Perfume Factory

This museum explains how perfumes are made, and sells famous name fragrances such as Chanel, Givenchy and Yves Saint-Laurent, plus local products.

✉ 393 York Road ☎ 905/685-6666

Ottawa
Boutique Le Papillon

Women's designer clothes from all over the world carefully selected and sold by knowledgeable salespeople.

✉ 136 Bank Street ☎ 613/233-1003 ◉ Closed Sun

Thunder Bay
Joyce Seppala Designs

Inspired by Canada's northern landscapes, Joyce Seppala designs stunning clothes in fleece fabrics that are both practical and fun.

✉ 508 East Victoria Avenue ☎ 807/624-0022 ◉ Closed Sun

Toronto
Algonquians Sweet Grass Gallery

Gallery owned by the Ojibwa. Exquisite sculptures in antler and soapstone, porcupine-quill jewelry, moccasins, dream catchers and other traditional crafts.

✉ 668 Queen Street West ☎ 416/703-1336 ◉ Osgoode then streetcar 501 west ◉ Closed Sun

Bounty

Sells contemporary ceramics, glass and jewelry, as well as objects made of wood and fiber, many created by the craftspeople who have their studios in the complex.

✉ Harbourfront Centre, 235 Queens Quay West ☎ 416/973-4993

Dr. Fleas

Undercover craft market north of the city with about 400 vendors selling all manner of objects. Farmers' market in summer.

✉ 8 Westmore Drive ☎ 416/745-3532 ◉ Sat–Sun only ◉ Union then bus 73

Eskimo Art Gallery

Very large collection of Inuit soapstone sculpture on display in a gallery reminiscent of the Arctic, with iceberg and tundra decorations and icy-blue lighting.

✉ 12 Queens Quay West ☎ 416/336-3000 ◉ Union then Harbourfront streetcar 509 or 510

Holt Renfrew

Holt's is exclusive, fashionable, expensive and patronized by the rich and powerful. Very chic café for lunch.

✉ 50 Bloor Street ☎ 416/922-2333 ◉ Bay

Tilley Endurables

Northeast of downtown, this is the flagship store of a Canadian business which made its name making hats (► panel), now sold all over North America. They specialize in tough, practical clothing of all types for outdoor activities and travel.

✉ 900 Don Mills Road (two blocks north of Eglinton) ☎ 416/441-6141 ◉ Eglinton then bus 34 followed by 35

The Tilley Hat

In 1980, Alex Tilley couldn't find a decent sailing hat, so he invented one. Tilley hats are handcrafted in Canada from strong, soft, cotton duck, which is specially treated to make it water-repellent and mildew-proof. The hats can be stuffed in a bag or pocket, they float – at least in salt water – and they come with a lifetime guarantee. Canadian forces wore Tilley hats during the 1991 Gulf War, and continue to be issued them wherever they serve – soldiers from other nations will do nearly anything to get one!

Where to Take the Children

Museum Programs
Most museums organize programs for children in the summer vacation and on weekends, which can take the form of workshops or special tours. It is worthwhile checking what is available when you are in a particular locality. Tourist offices can help you, as can the institutions themselves.

Atlantic Provinces

Bouctouche, New Brunswick
Le Pays de la Sangouine
La Sangouine, a bewitching old lady, takes kids around this re-created village while recounting stories. Mostly in French with some English tours and colorful musical shows. Traditional restaurant.
✉ 57 Acadie Street ☎ 506/743-1400 ◉ Daily, Jun to mid-Oct 🖱 Expensive

Cavendish, Prince Edward Island
Avonlea
The "Anne" books by Lucy Maud Montgomery were set on PEI (➤ 40). Children can relive the stories, explore the farm, take wagon rides and attend an old-fashioned school. Tearoom.
✉ Route 6 ☎ 902/963-3050 ◉ Daily, mid-Jun to Sep 🖱 Expensive

Fredericton, New Brunswick
Science East
Full of hands-on exhibits. Children can step inside a giant kaleidoscope, leave their shadow on a wall or see their hair stand on end in the static electricity display.
✉ 668 Brunswick Street ☎ 506/457-2340 ◉ Daily; closed Jan 🖱 Inexpensive

New Glasgow, Nova Scotia
Magic Valley Fun Park
Theme park with huge water slides, pedal and bumper boats, train ride, karting and live animals. At Storybook Village, young children can enjoy nursery rhymes.
✉ Highway 104 ☎ 902/396-4467 ◉ Jun to mid-Oct 🖱 Expensive

St. John's, Newfoundland
Fluvarium
Windows below water level show the life of a real stream full of trout, frogs and tadpoles. Feeding time 4 pm.
✉ Nagles Place, Pippy Park ☎ 709/754-3474 ◉ Daily, May–Sep; Mon–Fri, rest of year 🖱 Inexpensive

Québec

Granby
Granby Zoo
Large zoo with more than 800 animals of every variety, including elephants, giraffes, camels, bears and gorillas. Animal rides for children; water park. Food outlets.
✉ 525 rue Saint-Hubert ☎ 450/372-9113 ◉ Daily, end May–Aug; Sat–Sun, Sep to mid-Oct 🖱 Very expensive

Montebello
Parc Omega
North of Montebello. Drive-through enclosure where you can see buffalo, moose and bear in their natural habitats. On foot, you can explore the deer enclosure, otter pool and birds of prey area. Restaurant.
✉ Route 323 ☎ 819/423-5487 ◉ Daily 🖱 Expensive

Montréal
Biodôme
Under one roof, you can visit a tropical jungle, the Laurentian forest, the Gulf of St. Lawrence and the polar world. These four American ecosystems have been re-created complete with animals, fish, birds and vegetation. Cafeteria.
✉ 4777 avenue Pierre du Coubertin ☎ 514/868-3000 ◉ Daily 🚇 Viau 🖱 Expensive

Biosphère
Innovative interactive displays concerned with water form the basis of this interpretive center in the former U.S. pavilion of Expo 67. Don't miss the view from the roof. Cafeteria.

🖂 160 chemin Tour-de-l'Île ☎ 514/283-5000 🟢 Daily 🚇 Jean-Drapeau 🔖 Moderate

Centre des sciences de Montréal
Engrossing science center on the waterfront in the Old Port of Montréal. Hands-on exhibits, interactive movie and an IMAX movie theater. Cafeteria.

🖂 quai King Edward ☎ 514/496-4724 🟢 Daily; closed Mon in winter 🚇 Place d'Armes then short walk 🔖 Expensive

Québec City
Aquarium de Québec
West of the city. Outdoor habitats for polar bears and seals, walk-through tunnel in a huge tank with hundreds of marine animals, pavilion with thousands of fish. Restaurant.

🖂 1675 avenue des Hôtels ☎ 418/659-5264 🟢 Daily 🔖 Very expensive

Ontario

Cambridge
African Lion Safari
Southwest of Toronto. Home to more than 1,000 African animals – including lions, elephants, giraffes and monkeys – which roam freely in large game reserves that you can drive through or view from the safari bus.

🖂 Safari Road, Rural Route 1 ☎ 519/623-2620 🟢 Daily, late Apr to mid-Oct 🔖 Expensive

Children's Museum
The first museum in Canada specifically devoted to kids. Experience life in the Arctic, dig up dinosaur bones, hunt for cave dwellers, or dress up like an astronaut.

🖂 21 Wharncliffe Road South ☎ 519/434-5726 🟢 Daily 🔖 Inexpensive

Niagara Falls
Marineland
Huge aquarium complex with performing beluga whales, orcas, sea lions and walruses. Children can help feed the animals and there are thrill rides. Cafeterias.

🖂 7657 Portage Road ☎ 905/356-9565 🟢 Daily, late Jun to mid-Oct 🚌 Niagara People Mover bus (Mar–Dec) 🔖 Very expensive

Ottawa
Aboriginal Experiences
On an island that has been a place of aboriginal celebration for centuries. Brings aboriginal culture to life with tepees, totem poles, canoes, singing, dancing and storytelling. Restaurant with traditional aboriginal food.

🖂 12 Stirling Avenue, Victoria Island ☎ 613/564-9494 🟢 Daily, mid-Jun to Sep 🔖 Moderate

Valleyview Little Animal Farm
Just west of Ottawa. Farm animals of all types, train ride, puppet shows, variety of old farm equipment. Best in spring, when there are lots of baby animals. Café.

🖂 4750 Fallowfield Road, Nepean ☎ 613/591-1126 🟢 Tue–Sun, Mar–Oct 🔖 Inexpensive

Toronto
Centreville
Centered around a re-created Ontario village of 100 years ago. Amusement park with a Ferris wheel, log flume, antique carousel, bumper cars, plus rides on boats, a train and ponies. Fast food.

🖂 Centre Island ☎ 416/203-0405 🟢 Daily, mid-May to early Sep; Sat–Sun, early May and late Sep 🔖 Admission free, rides expensive

National Museums in Ottawa
All the national museums in Ottawa (➤ 70–71) organize programs specifically for children. One particularly good program is offered by the Canadian Museum of Nature, which is located in the Victoria Memorial Building at 240 McLeod Street (☎ 613/566-4700). In its Exploration Section, children can pick up and examine items, as well as marvel at huge dinosaur skeletons, animal dioramas and a creepy critters gallery.

Theaters & Nightclubs

Atlantic Provinces
Casino
Halifax's waterfront Casino Nova Scotia, at 1983 Upper Water Street (☎ 902/425-7777), offers baccarat, blackjack, craps, poker and roulette on the tables. It also has slot machines and live entertainment daily, year-round.

Atlantic Provinces

Annapolis Royal, Nova Scotia
King's
Live theater, concerts and movies presented year-round in a historic building on the town's main street. Also a summer festival.
✉ 209 St. George Street
☎ 902/532-7704

Charlottetown, Prince Edward Island
Olde Dublin Pub
Irish pub open year-round, with live entertainment and traditional music Sat–Sun, May–Sep.
✉ 131 Sydney Street
☎ 902/892-6992

Fredericton, New Brunswick
Dolan's
Irish pub presenting East Coast Celtic performers Thu–Sat nights and rock shows Sun–Wed nights, year-round. Also has a full dinner menu.
✉ Piper's Lane, 349 King Street
☎ 506/454-7474

The Playhouse
Next to the Provincial Legislature. Theater presenting drama, comedy and all kinds of musical performances year-round.
✉ 686 Queen Street ☎ 506/458-8344

Halifax, Nova Scotia
Grafton Street Dinner Theatre
Specializes in lighthearted musical comedies served up during dinner by staff in costume. Audience participation encouraged.
✉ 1741 Grafton Street
☎ 902/425-1961

Lower Deck Pub
Traditional Maritimes music in a former privateers' warehouse every night year-round.
✉ Historic Properties, Lower Water Street ☎ 902/425-1501

Neptune
Famous Canadian theater company presenting drama, music and comedy in two auditoriums year-round.
✉ 1593 Argyle Street
☎ 902/429-7070

Wolfville, Nova Scotia
Atlantic Theatre Festival
On Acadia University campus. Theater classics presented Jul–Aug by performers from all over the world.
✉ 356 Main Street ☎ 902/542-4242

Québec

Montréal
Centaur Theatre
Offers a regular season (Sep–May) of professional English theater in the former stock exchange building in Old Montréal.
✉ 453 rue St-François-Xavier
☎ 514/288-3161 🚇 Place d'Armes

Comedyworks
On the second floor of Jimbo's Pub. There's comedy shows every night, improv comedy during the week and big-name shows on weekends.
✉ 1238 rue Bishop ☎ 514/398-9661 🚇 Guy-Concordia, Lucien L'Allier

Complexe Bourbon
In the heart of Montréal's Gay Village. Huge complex covering an entire city block,

with a disco, restaurants, hotel, sauna and bathhouse. Promotes itself as the biggest gay establishment in the world.

⊠ 1474–1574 rue Ste-Catherine Est ☎ 514/529-6969 Ⓜ Beaudry

House of Jazz/Maison de Jazz
► 94

Le Festin du Gouverneur
Historical comedy (with more accent on the comedy) performed by staff dressed in period costumes as you dine in the former barracks building of the old fort (year-round).

⊠ Fort de l'Île Ste-Hélène, Parc Jean-Drapeau ☎ 514/879-1141 Ⓜ Jean-Drapeau

Place des Arts
Montréal's major performing arts center, with a concert hall, two large and two small theaters, and the Museum of Contemporary Art. Classical music, opera, ballet and live theater year-round.

⊠ 175 rue Ste-Catherine Ouest ☎ 514/842-2112 Ⓜ Place-des-Arts

Saidye Bronfman Centre
Theater in the Jewish cultural complex, with drama, comedy and music in English and Yiddish year-round (closed Sat).

⊠ 5170 rue Côte Ste-Catherine ☎ 514/739-2301 Ⓜ Côte Sainte-Catherine

North Hatley
The Piggery Theatre
In a former big barn in the Eastern Townships. Live theater and comedy in English Jun–Sep.

⊠ 215 chemin Simard, Route 108 ☎ 819/842-2431

Québec City
Café des Arts
In Upper Town. Café-club offering performances of mime and jazz, poetry readings, and traditional singing of *chansons* year-round.

⊠ 1000 rue St-Jean ☎ 418/694-1499

Grand Théâtre du Québec
Home to the Opéra du Québec and the Québec Symphony Orchestra. Full program of dance, music and theater (in French) year-round.

⊠ 269 boulevard René-Lévesque Est ☎ 418/643-8131

Ontario

Niagara-on-the-Lake
Shaw Festival Theatre
Theater primarily devoted to the production of the works of Irish writer George Bernard Shaw, the theater festival (Apr–Nov) also offers plays by other authors as well as comedy and musical shows.

⊠ 10 Queen's Parade ☎ 905/468-2172

Ottawa
D'Arcy McGee's
Centrally located pub, always lively with Celtic music from the Maritimes and from Ireland. Live music Wed–Sun, year-round.

⊠ 44 Sparks Street ☎ 613/230-4433

Duke of Somerset
Historic pub complex just south of downtown. Pub with live rock music from local bands as well as karaoke and traditional pub league games.

⊠ 352 Somerset Street ☎ 613/233-7762

Québec Casinos
The Casino de Montréal has a spectacular site on Île Notre-Dame in a building that originally housed France's pavilion at Expo 67, at 1 avenue du Casino (☎ 514/392-2746 Ⓜ Jean-Drapeau then free shuttle bus). There are five floors of gaming tables, slot machines and entertainment.

Just east of downtown Ottawa in Québec province is Gatineau's Casino du Lac-Leamy, at 1 boulevard du Casino (☎ 819/772-2100). The complex has gaming tables, slot machines, entertainment and a conference center, and is open year-round to over-18s.

Ontario Casinos

Niagara Falls has two casinos that both open daily, year-round. The Casino Niagara, at 5705 Falls Avenue (☎ 888/946-3255 toll-free), has gaming tables, slot machines, restaurants and shopping. The Niagara Fallsview Casino Resort, at Fallsview Boulevard (☎ 888/325-5788 toll-free), is a new complex overlooking the falls. It has 230,000sq m (2.5 million square feet) of gaming space, plus a hotel, health spa and shopping mall.

A short drive north of Toronto is the Casino Rama, on Rural Route 6, Rama (☎ 705/329-3325). It has a hotel and restaurants, as well as gaming tables and slot machines, and is open daily, year-round.

National Arts Centre

Huge performing arts center in the heart of the capital offering theater in both English and French, dance performances and classical and popular music shows year-round.

✉ 53 Elgin Street ☎ 613/947-7000

Zaphod Beeblebrox

In the Byward Market area. One of Ottawa's top live music and dance venues. Its name comes from a character in Douglas Adams' book, *The Hitchhiker's Guide to the Galaxy*.

✉ 27 York Street ☎ 613/562-1010

Stratford
Stratford Festival of Canada

Canada's premier English-language theater company, producing the works of William Shakespeare as well as other classics and musical comedies on four stages (May–Nov).

✉ 55 Queen Street ☎ 519/271-0055

Toronto
Elgin and Winter Garden Theatres

Beautifully restored "double-decker" theaters (the Elgin is downstairs, the Winter Garden above it) producing drama, music and comedy year-round.

✉ 189 Yonge Street ☎ 416/314-2871 🚇 Queen

The Guvernment

Club complex on the waterfront with seven different rooms offering big-name performers, local talent and DJs. For some shows, a dress code may apply. Fri–Sat nights, sometimes Thu nights in summer.

✉ 132 Queens Quay East
☎ 416/869-0045 🚇 Union then walk or bus 6 east

Healey's

Owned by singer-guitarist Jeff Healey, who performs regularly. Considered by many to be one of Toronto's best live music clubs. Tue–Sun, year-round.

✉ 178 Bathurst Street
☎ 416/703-5882 🚇 Osgoode then streetcar 501 west

Horseshoe

Club offering an eclectic mix of alternative rock, pop and contemporary country music daily, year-round.

✉ 370 Queen Street West
☎ 416/598-4226 🚇 Osgoode then short walk or streetcar 501 west to Spadina

Princess of Wales

Splendid theater built in the 1990s with a huge stage suitable for big productions such as *The Lion King*. Operates year-round.

✉ 300 King Street West
☎ 416/593-4142 🚇 St. Andrew

Royal Alexandra

Beautifully restored repertory theater in the Beaux-Arts style. Offers mainly musicals year-round.

✉ 260 King Street West
☎ 416/593-4142 🚇 St. Andrew

Yuk Yuk's Comedy Cabaret

Founded in Toronto in 1976 to promote Canadian talent; now a chain of comedy clubs across Canada. Shows daily, year-round.

✉ 224 Richmond Street West
☎ 416/967-6425 🚇 Osgoode then streetcar 501

Sports

Atlantic Provinces

Halifax, Nova Scotia
Halifax Mooseheads
The Mooseheads hockey team is not in the National Hockey League (NHL) but still has an enthusiastic following. Games Sep–Mar.
✉ **Halifax Metro Centre, 1800 Argyle Street** ☎ **902/451-1221**

Moncton, New Brunswick
Moncton Wildcats
Not in the NHL; they play the Mooseheads and teams from Québec Sep–Mar.
✉ **Moncton Coliseum, 377 Killam Drive** ☎ **506/857-4100**

Québec

Montréal
Montréal Alouettes
McGill University stadium is home to the Alouettes, who play in the Canadian Football League (Jun–Nov).
✉ **Percival Molson Stadium, 475 avenue des Pins** ☎ **514/871-2266** 🚇 **McGill then free pre-game shuttle**

Montréal Canadiens
They say that hockey is not a sport in Montréal but a religion. It's fast, furious and exciting. The famous "Habs," as the Canadiens are called locally, have won the coveted Stanley Cup (► side panel) almost twice as many times as any other team (Sep–early Apr; Stanley Cup playoffs Apr–May if team qualifies).
✉ **Bell Centre, 1260 rue de la Gauchetière** ☎ **514/790-1245** 🚇 **Bonaventure, Lucien L'Allier**

Montréal Expos
Only two Canadian teams play major league baseball, the Expos being one of them. Home games are played in the Olympic Stadium (► 49), which is worth seeing inside even if you are not a baseball fan (Apr–Oct).
✉ **Olympic Stadium, 4549 avenue Pierre du Coubertin** ☎ **514/846-3976** 🚇 **Pie IX**

Ontario

Ottawa
Ottawa Senators
Part of the National Hockey League, the Senators also play home games in the Corel Centre (Sep–early Apr; Stanley Cup playoffs Apr–May if team qualifies).
✉ **Corel Centre, 1000 Palladium Drive, Kanata** ☎ **613/599-0250**

Toronto
Toronto Argonauts
The Argonauts play in the Canadian Football League (Jun–Nov) and hold the record for number of victories.
✉ **SkyDome, 1 Blue Jays Way** ☎ **416/341-2700** 🚇 **Union then Skywalk**

Toronto Blue Jays
One of only two major league baseball teams in Canada. They have won the World Series twice and have a loyal following (Apr–Oct).
✉ **SkyDome, 1 Blue Jays Way** ☎ **905/341-1234** 🚇 **Union then Skywalk**

Toronto Maple Leafs
There's always lots of excitement and big crowds when the Maple Leafs are playing at home, especially if they happen to be up against the Montréal Canadiens (regular season Sep–early Apr; Stanley Cup playoffs Apr–May if team qualifies).
✉ **Air Canada Centre, 40 Bay Street** ☎ **416/815-5700** 🚇 **Union**

The Stanley Cup
The regular hockey season (Sep–early Apr) finishes with the playoffs for the Stanley Cup, the oldest trophy competed for by professional athletes in North America. The cup was donated to the sport in 1892 by Lord Stanley of Preston, Governor General of Canada. Today, only teams that are members of the National Hockey League (NHL) can compete for the coveted trophy. There are 30 teams in the NHL, six of them Canadian. The Montréal Canadiens have won a record 23 Stanley Cups since the formation of the NHL in 1917 (they also won in 1916), while the Toronto Maple Leafs are in second place with 13 wins.

Lacrosse
Despite the prominence of ice hockey, lacrosse is officially Canada's national sport. The Ottawa Rebel play this fast and furious game at the Corel Centre west of Ottawa Dec–Apr (1000 Palladium Drive, Kanata ☎ 613/599-0100).

What's On When

Festival Nation
The festivals and events listed here are the best known and most established in Eastern Canada, although almost every community organizes some kind of celebration during the summer months – for example, Canada Day on July 1 is universally celebrated. It is therefore worthwhile inquiring locally about what might be happening when you are visiting a particular area.

January
Niagara Icewine Celebrations, Niagara Peninsula
Winterlude, Ottawa

February
Québec Winter Carnival, Québec City
Montréal High Lights Festival, Montréal
Wintercity, Toronto

March
Sno-Break Winter Festival, Goose Bay, Labrador
Toronto Flower and Garden Show, Toronto

April
Blue Metropolis Literary Festival, Montréal
World Stage International Theatre Festival, Toronto

May
Milk International Children's Festival of the Arts, Toronto
Canadian Tulip Festival, Ottawa

June
Canadian Grand Prix (Formula 1), Montréal
Québec national holiday (Jun 24), Québec
Canada Dance Festival, Ottawa

June/July
Festival 500, Sharing the Voices, St. John's
Nova Scotia International Tattoo, Halifax
Rollo Bay Fiddle Festival, Prince Edward Island
International Jazz Festival, Montréal
Fêtes du Québec maritime, Bas-St-Laurent, Québec
Montréal International Fireworks Competition, Montréal

July
Canada's Irish Festival, Miramichi, New Brunswick
Just for Laughs Comedy Festival, Montréal
Festival d'été du Québec, Québec City
Les Grands Feux Loto Québec, Montmorency, Québec
Festival de Lanaudière, Joliette, Québec
Divers/Cité – International Gay & Lesbian Pride Festival, Montréal
Kingston Buskers Rendezvous, Kingston

August
Halifax International Busker Festival, Halifax
Atlantic Seafood Festival, Moncton, New Brunswick
Fergus Scottish Festival and Highland Games, Fergus, Ontario
Festival of the Islands, Gananoque, Ontario
Canadian National Exhibition, Toronto
Canadian Grand Masters Fiddle Championship, Nepean, Ottawa

September
Harvest Jazz and Blues Festival, Fredericton
Niagara Grape and Wine Festival, St. Catharines, Ontario

October
Celtic Colours Festival, Sydney, Nova Scotia
Oktoberfest, Kitchener, Ontario

November
Canadian Aboriginal Festival, Toronto

December
Christmas Lights Across Canada, Ottawa

Practical Matters

Above: *a ferry boat glides past downtown Toronto*
Right: *phone booth*

TIME DIFFERENCES

Ottawa (EST) 12 noon	New York 12 noon	Los Angeles 9AM	London 5PM	Tokyo 2AM	Sydney 5AM

BEFORE YOU GO

WHAT YOU NEED

	UK	USA	Europe
● Required ○ Suggested ▲ Not required — Some countries require a passport to remain valid for a minimum period (usually at least six months) beyond the date of entry – contact their consulate or embassy or your travel agent for details.			
Passport	●	○	●
Visa (regulations can change – check before your journey)	▲	▲	▲
Return Ticket	○	○	○
Health Inoculation	●	▲	●
Travel Insurance	○	○	○
Driving License	●	●	●
Car Insurance Certificate	●	●	●
Car Registration	●	●	●

WHEN TO GO

Montréal

High season

Low season

-8°C	-7°C	-1°C	7°C	17°C	23°C	26°C	25°C	21°C	13°C	6°C	1°C
JAN	FEB	MAR	APR	MAY	JUN	JUL	AUG	SEP	OCT	NOV	DEC

Sunshine & showers   Cloud   Sun   Snow & Ice

TOURIST OFFICES

In the U.S.A.
Canadian Tourism Commission
✉ 550 South Hope Street, 9th Floor, Los Angeles, CA 90071-2627
☎ 323/937-7021; fax: 323/937-5657

Canadian Tourism Commission
✉ 2625 Piedmont Road, Suite 56–333, Atlanta, GA 30324
☎ 404/315-0028; fax: 404/315-4801

In the U.K.
Canadian Tourism Commission
✉ Visit Canada, PO Box 170, Ashford, Kent TN24 0ZX
☎ (0906) 871 5000

In Australia
Canadian Tourism Commission
✉ Suite 105, Jones Bay Wharf, 19–21 Pirrama Road, Pyrmont, NSW 2009
☎ (02) 9571 1665; fax: (02) 9571 1766

EMERGENCY TELEPHONE NUMBERS
For police, fire and ambulance services in Ontario, Québec, New Brunswick and Newfoundland and Labrador: dial 911. In Prince Edward Island and Nova Scotia: dial 0 for the operator and say that it is an emergency.

WHEN YOU ARE THERE

ARRIVING

Eastern Canada's major airports are in Toronto and Montréal; most visitors arrive at one or the other. There are smaller airports in Ottawa, Québec, Halifax and St. John's. The major Canadian airline is Air Canada ☎ 888/247-2262 toll-free; www.aircanada.ca

Toronto International Airport	**Journey times**
Miles from city center	
17 miles	🚗 45 minutes
	🚌 45 minutes
	🚌 1–1.5 hours

Montréal International Airport	**Journey times**
Miles from city center	
9 miles	🚗 30 minutes
	🚌 30 minutes

MONEY

Eastern Canada's currency is the Canadian dollar (1 dollar = 100 cents). The Canadian $1 and $2 bills no longer exist, but there are $5, $10, $20, $50 and $100 bills (the $100 bill is sometimes difficult to use because people are suspicious of it owing to forgeries). Coins come as pennies (1 cent), nickels (5 cents), dimes (10 cents), quarters (25 cents), loonies ($1; so called because of the bird on them), and twonies ($2). The $1 coin is gold-colored, while the $2 coin has a gold center and silver rim. Exchange rates are notoriously variable, so it is wise to check the current rate just before leaving on a trip.

TIME

 Eastern Canada has four different time zones. Most of Ontario and Québec observe Eastern Standard Time (EST). The most westerly part of Ontario observes Central Standard Time (EST -1). New Brunswick, Nova Scotia, PEI, Labrador, and part of eastern Québec observe Atlantic Standard Time (EST +1). The island section of Newfoundland observes Newfoundland Standard Time (1.5 hours ahead of EST).

CUSTOMS

 YES
Goods obtained duty-free for import from any country into Eastern Canada (provided you are over 18):
200 cigarettes, 50 cigars or 400g (just over 8oz) of tobacco
1L bottle (40fl oz) of wine or spirits
24 regular-size cans or bottles of beer
Dogs, cats and other pets, but they must have been vaccinated against rabies within the preceding 12-month period and you must carry the vaccination certificate with you.

NO Plants, flowers or other vegetation; illegal drugs; obscene material; firearms and ammunition, except for hunting trips (have documentation with you).

119

EMBASSIES & CONSULATES

U.S.A.
613/238-5335
www.usembassy
canada.gov

U.K.
613/237-1303
www.britainin-
canada.org

AUSTRALIA
613/236-0841
www.ahc-
ottawa.org

FRANCE
613/789-1795
www.ambafranc
e-ca.org/english

GERMANY
613/232-1101
www.germanem-
bassyottawa.org

WHEN YOU ARE THERE

TOURIST OFFICES

- **Tourism New Brunswick**
  ✉ P.O. Box 12345, Campbellton, New Brunswick, E3N 3T6
  ☎ 800/561-0123 toll-free; www.tourismnb.ca

- **Newfoundland and Labrador Department of Tourism**
  ✉ P.O. Box 8700, St. John's, Newfoundland and Labrador, A1B 4J6
  ☎ 800/563-6353 toll-free; www.gov.nf.ca/tourism

- **Nova Scotia Tourism**
  ✉ P.O. Box 456, 1800 Argyle Street, Halifax, Nova Scotia, B3J 2R5
  ☎ 800/565-0000 toll-free; www.novascotia.com

- **Ontario Travel**
  ✉ 10th Floor, Hearst Block, 900 Bay Street, Toronto, Ontario, M7A 2E1
  ☎ 800/668-2746 toll-free; www.ontariotravel.net

- **Prince Edward Island Department of Tourism**
  ✉ P.O. Box 940, Charlottetown, Prince Edward Island, C1A 7M5
  ☎ 888/734-7529 toll-free; www.peiplay.com

- **Tourisme Québec**
  ✉ P.O. Box 979, Montréal, Québec, H3C 2W3
  ☎ 877/266-5687 toll-free; www.bonjourquebec.com

PUBLIC HOLIDAYS

1 Jan New Year's Day
Mar 17 St. Patrick's Day (Newfoundland and Labrador)
Mar–Apr Good Friday
Mar–Apr Easter Monday
Apr 23 St. George's Day (Newfoundland and Labrador)
May (Mon closest to 24) Victoria Day
Jun 24 St-Jean-Baptiste Day (Québec)
Jun 24 Discovery Day (Newfoundland and Labrador)
Jul 1 Canada Day
Jul 12 Orangeman's Day (Newfoundland and Labrador)
Aug (1st Mon) New

Brunswick Day (New Brunswick)
Aug (1st Mon) Civic holiday (Ontario)
Aug (1st Mon) Natal Day (Nova Scotia, except in Halifax, usually Jul or Aug)
Aug (1st Mon) Natal Day (PEI – by proclamation)
Aug Regatta Day/civic holiday (Newfoundland and Labrador – fixed by municipal council orders)
Sep (1st Mon) Labour Day
Oct (2nd Mon) Thanksgiving (note: this is not at the same time as American Thanksgiving)
Nov 11 Remembrance Day (not celebrated in Québec)
Dec 25 and Dec 26

OPENING HOURS

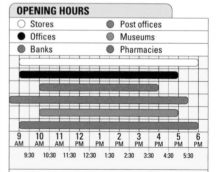

Stores: Mon–Fri 9–6 (until 9 Thu and Fri), Sat 9–5, Sun noon–5. Some stores do not open on Sun. Supermarkets often have longer hours.
Offices: Mon–Fri 9–5 (government offices until 4).
Banks: Mon–Fri 10–4. Some open earlier, and some stay open to 5 or 6 on Thu or Fri.
Post offices: Mon–Fri 8:30–5:30. May stay open later than 5:30 and open Sat am.
Museums: Tue–Sun 10–5. Art museums often open at 11. Most are closed Mon, and major stay open until 9 one evening a week.

DRIVE ON THE
RIGHT

TOILETS
FREE

PUBLIC TRANSPORTATION

 Internal Flights Air Canada (☎ 888/247-2262 toll-free; www.aircanada.ca; subsidiaries Air Canada Jazz and Air Canada Tango), is the region's major carrier. WestJet (☎ 403/250-5839, 888/937-8538 toll-free; www.westjet.com) offers services in Ontario and the Atlantic provinces.

 Trains VIA Rail (☎ 888/842-7245 toll-free; www.viarail.ca) provides most rail passenger services in Eastern Canada. There are excellent daily services between Montréal and Toronto, Montréal and Québec, Montréal and Ottawa. Trains run several times a week between Montréal and Gaspé, and Montréal and Halifax.

 Long-distance Buses This is the least expensive option and gives access to most of the region. Greyhound Canada (☎ 800/661-8747 toll-free; www.greyhound.ca) serves Ontario, with cross-border links to U.S. cities. Voyageur (☎ 514/842-2281; www.voyageur.com) serves Québec and the Atlantic provinces.

 Ferries In Nova Scotia, services link Yarmouth with the state of Maine, Digby with Saint John, New Brunswick, and Caribou with Wood Islands, Prince Edward Island. The Nova Scotia Tourist Office (see opposite) can supply details. Newfoundland is linked to North Sydney, Nova Scotia by two different ferries run by Maine Atlantic (www.marine-atlantic.ca).

 Urban Transportation Toronto and Montréal have excellent subway systems. The Toronto Transit System (TTC ☎ 416/393-4636; www.ttc.ca), operates buses, streetcars, the subway and a light rapid transit system (LTR). The Société de Transport de Montréal (STM ☎ 514/288-6287; www.stm.info), runs the métro and bus service.

CAR RENTAL

 All the major car-rental companies are represented in Eastern Canada (Avis, Budget, Dollar, Hertz, National, and Thrifty). You must be over 21 years, and produce identification and a valid driver's license (which you have held for at least a year).

TAXIS

 Taxis are the most expensive option. Fares mount quickly, especially in rush-hour traffic. Cabs can be found in stands beside major hotels, at airports and train and bus stations or can be hailed on the street or called by telephone.

DRIVING

 Speed limits on expressways: 100kph (60mph)

 Speed limits on other major roads: 70–90kph (40–55mph)

 Speed limits in urban areas and on rural routes: 50kph (30mph) or less

 Must be worn by all persons in a vehicle (drivers and passengers) in both the front and back seats

 Random breath-testing. Never drive under the influence of alcohol.

 Unleaded gasoline is heavily taxed (leaded gasoline has been phased out). Gas stations stay open until 9–10 pm (some all night). Away from the much-traveled south, gas stations may be far apart and close at 8 pm.

If you intend to drive long distances in remote areas, take out a membership in the Canadian Automobile Association (☎ 800/222-4357 toll-free; www.caa.ca). They or their local affiliate can help in case of breakdown. If you are a member of AAA, you are entitled to full service with the CAA if you have your membership card with you.

PERSONAL SAFETY

Although Eastern Canada is remarkably crime-free, reasonable caution should be exercised and a few simple precautions will help prevent unfortunate incidents:

- Don't leave bags or other valuables visible in your car; instead, put everything in the trunk.
- Don't wear expensive jewelry or carry large sums of money on you.
- In the major cities where there is a danger of pickpockets, consider carrying your passport and credit cards in a pouch or belt.
- Walk along only well-lit streets at night.

The Royal Canadian Mounted Police (RCMP; www.rcmp-grc.gc.ca) is the federal police force. The "Mounties" also ensure regular police work in all four Atlantic provinces. When on duty, RCMP officers look just like any other police force and drive cars (the red jackets, Stetsons, and horses are used only for ceremonies).
Police assistance: ☎ 911 (except in Prince Edward Island and Nova Scotia – dial 0).

TELEPHONES

Outdoor public telephones are located in glass and metal booths. To make a call, lift the handset, insert the correct coin (25¢ or $1), a telephone credit card or a prepaid calling card (available from post offices, convenience stores and newsagents), then dial.
The toll-free numbers listed in this guide are free only when calling from within North America.

International Dialing Codes	
From Canada to:	
U.S.A.:	**1**
U.K.:	**011 44**
Australia:	**011 61**
France:	**011 33**
Germany:	**011 49**
Italy:	**011 39**
Netherlands:	**011 31**
Spain:	**011 34**

MAIL

Mail boxes are generally red, with the words "Canada Post" or "Postes Canada" written on them. For hours of post offices, ► 120.

ELECTRICITY

The electricity voltage across Eastern Canada is 110 volts (the same as in the U.S.A.).

Sockets require plugs with two flat prongs (occasionally three flat prongs). Visitors arriving from outside North America will require an adapter as well a voltage converter.

TIPS/GRATUITIES

Yes ✓ No ✗		
Restaurants (where service not included)	✓	10–15%
Cafés (where service not included)	✓	10%
Hotel service staff	✓	10%
Hairdressers	✓	10%
Taxis	✓	10%
Tour guides	✓	$1
Cinema attendants	✗	
Cloakroom attendants	✓	$1
Washrooms/restrooms	✗	

PHOTOGRAPHY

When to photograph: The best light for photography is generally early morning or evening. Be careful with lighting when taking photos in the snow, as the reflections of the sun on the snow can be incredibly bright.

Where to buy film: Many convenience stores and pharmacies sell regular film, as do specialized camera stores.

Restrictions: Certain museums ban photography completely, and practically all forbid the use of flash.

HEALTH

Insurance Visitors requiring treatment while in Canada must pay for it, which can be expensive. It is essential to take out health insurance. Your own insurance company is the best source of advice on what is best for you. Make sure you keep all bills and receipts to make a claim. And make sure your coverage includes a "repatriation" clause in case no suitable treatment is available.

Dental Services If you require dental help (expensive), ask at the reception desk of your hotel. Most hotels keep a list of dentists and medical centers handy. Otherwise, try the local tourist office or the Yellow Pages.

Sun Advice Ontario and Québec have hot weather in midsummer, with temperatures climbing to the 30s °C (80s and 90s °F), so use sunscreen. The winter sun reflected off the snow can cause serious sunburn; use sunblock or sunscreen during outdoor activities such as skiing.

Prescription Drugs Carry a full supply of any prescription drug that you have to take. Over-the-counter drugs are readily available in pharmacies, but no Canadian pharmacy will accept an out-of-province prescription. Should you run out of or lose your supply of prescription drugs, you will have to visit a Canadian doctor to get a new prescription that is recognized locally.

Water It is perfectly safe to drink tap water in any part of eastern Canada. Bottled water is also widely available. When camping, boil drinking water to protect yourself against "beaver fever." This comes from the parasite *Giardia lamblia*, which thrives in small streams and lakes.

CONCESSIONS

Students Full-time students can benefit from certain reductions at museums and other tourist attractions. Students should carry their student card or be prepared to prove their age.

Seniors Most museums and tourist attractions offer reduced rates for seniors (ages vary from 55 to 60 to 65). If this affects you, it is best to ask. You will have to be prepared to prove your age. Public transportation systems also offer reductions for seniors, but in some cities this applies only to local residents; once again, you will have to ask.

CLOTHING SIZES

U.K.	Rest of Europe	Canada/U.S.A.	
36	46	36	
38	48	38	
40	50	40	Suits
42	52	42	
44	54	44	
46	56	46	
7	41	8	
7.5	42	8.5	
8.5	43	9.5	Shoes
9.5	44	10.5	
10.5	45	11.5	
11	46	12	
14.5	37	14.5	
15	38	15	
15.5	39/40	15.5	Shirts
16	41	16	
16.5	42	16.5	
17	43	17	
8	34	6	
10	36	8	
12	38	10	Dresses
14	40	12	
16	42	14	
18	44	16	
4.5	38	6	
5	38	6.5	
5.5	39	7	Shoes
6	39	7.5	
6.5	40	8	
7	41	8.5	

WHEN DEPARTING

- It is advisable to contact your airline two days prior to departure to reconfirm your flight and to ensure that the flight details remain unchanged. For international flights, arrive at the airport two hours before take-off (or the check-in time requested by your airline).
- Remember that line-ups to pass through security can be long at major airports (notably Toronto).

LANGUAGE

The official language of the province of Québec is French. Most sights in the book are listed by their French name, followed by the English translation. For a few sights the English name is given first when this is in common use.
A considerable number of people in Ontario, New Brusnwick and PEI also speak French as their mother tongue, so it helps to know a few words of the language.

hotel/inn	*hôtel/auberge*	double room	*occupation double*
bed-and-breakfast	*gîte touristique*	one night	*une nuit*
single room	*occupation simple*	room service	*service à la chambre*

bank	*banque*	banknote	*billet de banque*
exchange office	*bureau de change*	check	*chèque*
post office	*bureau de poste*	traveler's check	*chèque de voyage*
coin	*pièce de monnaie*	credit card	*carte de credit*

restaurant	*restaurant*	waiter	*serveur*
café	*café*	The check,	*L'addition s'il*
pub/bar	*brasserie / bar*	please	*vous plaît*
breakfast/lunch/dinner	*déjeuner/dîner/souper*	washrooms/restrooms	*toilettes*
table	*table*		
menu	*menu/table d'hôte*		

airport/airplane	*aéroport/avion*	entrance/exit	*entrée/sortie*
ferry/port	*traversier/port*	right/left	*droite/gauche*
customs/international border	*douanes/frontière*	straight ahead	*à droite*
expressway/road/street	*autoroute/chemin/rue*	north/south/east/west	*nord/sud/est/ouest*
stop (road sign)	*arrêt*	morning/	*matin/*
subway/bus/taxi	*métro/autobus/taxi*	afternoon	*après-midi*
station/train/tickets	*gare/train/billets*	evening/night	*soir/nuit*

hello	*bonjour*	you're welcome	*bienvenue*
good evening/	*bonsoir/*	please	*s'il vous plaît*
good night	*bon nuit*	Excuse me	*Excusez-moi*
goodbye	*au revoir*	How much?	*Combien?*
yes/no	*oui/non*	open/closed	*ouvert/fermé*
thank you/	*merci/*		

INDEX

Acknowledgments

The Automobile Association would like to thank the following libraries, agencies and photographers for their assistance in the preparation of this book.

ALAMY 58br, 60c; ART GALLERY OF NOVA SCOTIA 33c; CANADA HIGH COMMISSION 32b; CIRQUE DE SOLIEL 14ct; © FORT WILLIAM HISTORICAL PARK 2; GETTY IMAGES 14cb, 14b; EMPICS 11c; JUST FOR LAUGHS FESTIVAL, MARTIN SAVARD 80c; LAKE SUPERIOR VISITS 13c; LES DESCENTES SUR LE ST-LAURENT 43, 44, 45t, 48t, 51, 53t, 54tl, 55t, 56t, 57t, 58t, 59t, 60t, 62t, 63t, 64t; MUSÉE D'ART CONTEMPORAIN DE MONTRÉAL, RICHARD-MAX TREMBLAY 48b; NATIONAL GALLERY OF CANADA 70b, 71c; NOVA SCOTIA TOURISM 42c, 58c, 80b; OLD PORT OF MONTRÉAL CORPORATION INC., A.P.E.S 51b; PHOTODISC 7c; RON GARNETT, COURTESY OF CONFEDERATION BRIDGE 40t; SCIENCE NORTH 23b; SUCRERIE DE LA MONTAGNE 59c; TOURISME MONTRÉAL 9c, 45b (Stéphan Poulin), 19b, 49, 50; UPPER CANADA VILLAGE 90c

The remaining photographs are held in the Association's own library (AA WORLD TRAVEL LIBRARY) and were taken by NICHOLAS SUMNER with the exception of the following:
PETE BENNETT 5b; JON DAVISON 8b, 17b, 74b, 85, 117t, 117b, 122t; JEAN-FRANÇOIS PIN 6ct, 7b, 10b, 16c, 22b, 24bl, 27b, 28, 29, 30t, 31t, 32t, 34t, 35, 37t, 39t, 42t, 46, 47, 53c, 56b, 57c, 58bl, 62c, 79b, 84, 91b; CLIVE SAWYER 122b

Dear Essential Traveller

**Your comments, opinions and recommendations are very
important to us. So please help us to improve our travel
guides by taking a few minutes to complete this simple
questionnaire.**

*You do not need a stamp (unless posted outside the UK). If you do not want to cut this page
from your guide, then photocopy it or write your answers on a plain sheet of paper.*

Send to: **The Editor, AA World Travel Guides,
FREEPOST SCE 4598, Basingstoke RG21 4GY.**

Your recommendations...

We always encourage readers' recommendations for restaurants, nightlife
or shopping – if your recommendation is used in the next edition of the
guide, we will send you a *FREE* AA *Essential* **Guide** of your choice.
Please state below the establishment name, location and your reasons
for recommending it.

_____
_____
_____
_____

Please send me **AA *Essential*** _____

About this guide...

Which title did you buy?
  AA *Essential* _____
Where did you buy it? _____
When? m m / y y

Why did you choose an AA *Essential* Guide? _____
_____
_____
_____
_____

Did this guide meet your expectations?
  Exceeded ☐   Met all ☐   Met most ☐   Fell below ☐
  Please give your reasons_____
_____
_____
_____

continued on next page...

Were there any aspects of this guide that you particularly liked? _____

_____

_____

Is there anything we could have done better? _____

_____

_____

About you...

Name (*Mr/Mrs/Ms*) _____

Address _____

_____

_____ Postcode _____

Daytime tel nos _____

Please only give us your mobile phone number if you wish to hear from us about other products and services from the AA and partners by text or mms.

Which age group are you in?
Under 25 ☐ 25–34 ☐ 35–44 ☐ 45–54 ☐ 55–64 ☐ 65+ ☐

How many trips do you make a year?
Less than one ☐ One ☐ Two ☐ Three or more ☐

Are you an AA member? Yes ☐ No ☐

About your trip...

When did you book? m m / y y   When did you travel? m m / y y

How long did you stay? _____

Was it for business or leisure? _____

Did you buy any other travel guides for your trip?
If yes, which ones? _____

Thank you for taking the time to complete this questionnaire. Please send it to us as soon as possible, and remember, you do not need a stamp (*unless posted outside the UK*).

Happy Holidays!

The Atlas

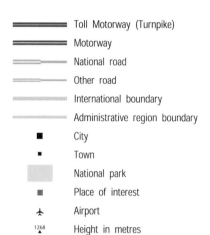

	Toll Motorway (Turnpike)
	Motorway
	National road
	Other road
	International boundary
	Administrative region boundary
■	City
▪	Town
	National park
■	Place of interest
✈	Airport
1268 ▲	Height in metres

130-133

0			300 km
0			200 miles

134-135

0		100 km
0		75 miles

Kuujjuaq

Labrador

North West River

Lake Melville

Hap
Vall
Goc

Mealy M

Caniapiscau

Schefferville

Smallwood Reservoir

Churchill

500

Menihek Lake

QUÉBEC

Lac Caniapiscau

Labrador City

Fermont

Lac Joseph

Lac Bienville

Lac Nichicun

Lac Naococane

Monts Otish

Réservoir Manicouagan

Lac Plétipi

Moisie

Harve
Saint-Pierre

Mingan

Rivière-au-Tonnerre

Rivière-St

Lac
Mistassini

Lac Manouane

Manicouagan

Sept-Îles

Gallix

Moisie

Port Menier

138

Parc National de Mistassini

Réservoir Pipmuacan

Port-Cartier

St Lawrence

Grande-Vallée

Gaspé

Mistassini

Lac Mistassini

Parc National d'Assinica

Mistassini

133

Chibougamau

Chapais

Parc Provincial de Chibougamau

Perihonca

Manicouagan

Ste-Anne-des-Monts

132

1268
Mont-Jacques Cartier

Murd

Godbout

Baie-Comeau

Chute-aux-Outardes

Matane

Parc de la Gaspésie

Bonave

New Richmond

167

Forestville

Mont-Joli

Luceville

Miguasha

Dalhousie

Lac-au-Saumon

Bath

Campbel

Lebel-sur-Quévillon

Lac
Mistassini

Parc Provincial d'Haute Maurice

Roberval

Desbiens

Le Bic

St-Fabien

Rimouski

Kedgwick

St-Quentin

NEW BRUNSW

Chibougamau

CHICOUTIMI JONQUIÈRE

Lac St-Jean

St-Joseph-de-la-Rive

Saguenay Fjord

Tadoussac

Ste Catherine

Edmundston

Ste-Anne-de-Madawaska

172

La Baie

Port-au-Persil

Rivière-du-Loup

Grand
Falls

Plaster

Val-Jalbert

Clermont

Les Éboulements

La Malbaie

St-Joseph-de-la-Rive

251

Woodstock

102

Réservoir Gouin

Parc Provencial des Laurentides

Baie-St-Paul

La Pocatière

St-Jean-Port-Joli

La Tuque

Charlevoix Coast

Montmagny

80

Sennetterre

155

QUÉBEC CITY

International Jean-Lesage

St-Apollinaire

Île d'Orléans

St-Raphaël

Vallée-Jonction

Val-d'Or

Réservoir Cabonga

Ste-Thècle

Beaupré

Beauceville

Inverness

Ste-Gédéon

USA

MAINE

Bangor
International

5

Parc Provincial de la Vérendrye

Parc du Mont Tremblant

St-Donat

TROIS-RIVIÈRES

Pierreville

Sorel

Victoriaville

Drummondville

Richmond

Lac-Mégantic

Augusta

Ste-Julienne

Bécancour

SHERBROOKE

105

Laurentians

Nicolet

Granby

Magog

Eastern Townships

Knowlton

NH

Auburn

130

St-Jérôme

International de Dorval

Laval

MONTREAL

Trans-Canada Highway

Ottawa

Deep River

A

Martawa

Pembroke

Canadian Museum of Civilzation

Gatineau

OTTAWA

Hawkesbury

Salaberry-de-Valleyfield

B

VERMONT

Plattsburgh

USA

C

Portl

A

B

C

1

2

3

4

5